HAUNTED BARTLESVILLE, OKLAHOMA

Also by Rita Cook

Published by The History Press:
A Brief History of Fort Worth
Haunted Fort Worth
Haunted Dallas

Published by Channel Lakes Publishing:
Tourist Town Guides: Fredericksburg, Texas

Published by Atlantic Publishing:
An Easy Guide to Understanding Robert's Rules of Order

Published by Publish America:
A Survival Guide for Independent Producers
Angel's Destiny (Fiction)

HAUNTED BARTLESVILLE, OKLAHOMA

RITA COOK

PHOTOGRAPHY BY RUSSELL W. DANDRIDGE

Haunted America

Published by Haunted America
A Division of The History Press
Charleston, SC 29403
www.historypress.net

First published 2012

Manufactured in the United States

ISBN 978.1.60949.506.0

Library of Congress CIP data applied for.

Notice: The information in this book is true and complete to the best of our knowledge. It is offered without guarantee on the part of the author or The History Press. The author and The History Press disclaim all liability in connection with the use of this book.

CONTENTS

Contents

FOREWORD

Author's Note: I met Bartlesville ghost hunter extraordinaire Scott Hickcock while in Bartlesville earlier this year on my fact-finding ghost mission. Scott, who had been in the military, really impressed me with his sixth sense, and we became fast friends. It is because of his belief in the other side and his assistance that I chose him to write this book's foreword.

A child who is barely five years old sits in the hallway, his back to the wall. He is playing with a toy airplane, his small hands gripping the fuselage. He pushes it back and forth. Darkness surrounds him; the only light that shines is from the kitchen doorway directly to his front.

The boy pretends he is flying. He is fascinated with airplanes. Then, as if from nowhere, a dark figure of a man appears to his left. Smiling, the boy asks, "Would you like to play with me?" The answer to the question comes in the form of silence.

"What is your name?" the boy asks. Again, there is no answer.

Perplexed, the boy frowns, gets up and walks through the kitchen into the living room where his grandmother sits watching television. She is watching Johnny Carson do his stand-up routine, and the boy enjoys the pleasure his grandmother gets from the show.

"Grandma, who is that man back there that has come to play with me?" the boy asks her. Fear shoots across the old woman's face. "What man, Scott?" she asks.

How strange, the boy thinks, that such a simple question would cause such fear. She takes him by the arm and puts him protectively behind her as she strides toward where the boy has been playing. She enters the kitchen and reaches into the drawer to her left where she keeps her pans. Grabbing the biggest one she can find, she turns the hallway light on and begins to search the four rooms in the back of the house, only to find that no one is there.

That is the first of many memories I have of the gift I have been given.

Many more similar instances have happened to me throughout my youth. I did not have any fear of ghosts though. I just didn't really understand why I was seeing and hearing the things that I did. I asked my family questions about this many times. They would either ignore me or chalk it up to a child's overactive imagination, but I knew better.

Growing up, there were very few people I could talk to about this. I learned that you could talk to God and that was acceptable. But if you saw or communicated with spirits or ghosts, you were taken to be a liar or just plain crazy. I find it a shame these days that we teach our children this. I have made sure not to make the same mistake with mine.

Why we should unlearn what is given to us at birth is beyond me. I have found that eyes that have not been taught to see or fear have the ability to see what our ancestors knew to be fact. Learned knowledge does not have to be the bane of our spirit. That is why children, animals and even our simple cameras have the ability to see what most adult minds refuse to fathom.

So please go through the pages of this book with an open mind. You may be surprised at what you see and even learn about yourself. I know I tried to ignore my gift on many occasions, but the longer I denied it, the more profound the events became when they happened.

Finally, at the age of thirty-two, I decided to become proactive, and so I called a local ghost team in to either prove my words or my insanity; whichever one it was, I was going to embrace it.

I knew I wasn't crazy.

The ghost hunters came with their cameras and tools of the trade, and I still feel that I made the right decision for me. What they captured on film is nothing short of amazing. Now, no longer filled with self-doubt, I have become more focused and do not so much control my talent as flow with its natural current. It brings me peace and has only guided my life in positive ways.

—Scott Hickcock

A Note from the Bartlesville Convention and Visitor's Bureau

Over the years, our community has welcomed travel writers from all over the world. These writers have helped share our stories of oil barons and Native Americans and have also written about our distinctive architecture. We are a place built on energy, agriculture and the pioneer spirit. We are Green Country.

At the heart of Oklahoma's Green Country is Bartlesville, an unexpected gem nestled next to the beautiful Osage Hills. Built on the history of the American West, Bartlesville is one of the state's most cosmopolitan cities. The town features numerous attractions, such as Price Tower, designed by Frank Lloyd Wright; the Woolaroc Wildlife Preserve and History Museum; and Discovery 1 Park, home of the Nellie Johnstone No. 1 and the site of Oklahoma's first commercial oil well. Other attractions, such as the Frank Phillips Home, Phillips Petroleum Company Museum and Bartlesville Area History Museum, continue to tell the story of how it all began.

Bartlesville's rich history has given the community an interesting array of characters, some of whom are said to still be hanging around. For this reason, the Bartlesville Convention and Visitor's Bureau was pleased to host Rita Cook during her research for this book. Longtime residents of Bartlesville have always known there were plenty of spooky stories,

A stone monument in downtown Bartlesville.

but no one had ever taken the time to put them all together. After all, what fun are ghosts without a good ghost story?

Some of our stories are tied to historic events while some are just legend and folklore, but all of them are a part of Bartlesville's colorful past. The Convention and Visitor's Bureau looks forward to sharing this book with visitors and locals alike. The growing popularity of haunted exploration and historic tourism go hand in hand. We hope everyone will enjoy learning more about the eerie tales and historic highlights of our corner of Oklahoma.

Special thanks to everyone who made this book a reality. There were many people who were willing to share stories. Many tourists come to Bartlesville for events or attractions and enthusiastically share all of the wonderful experiences they had and memories they made while visiting. We hope this book will entertain our guests and allow them to further enjoy their visit to Bartlesville.

Wherever your ghost hunting leads you, we hope you'll include northeast Oklahoma on your list of places to visit. For more information on Bartlesville, please visit our website at www.visitbartlesville.com or call us at 918-336-8708 or toll free at 1-800-364-8708.

Enjoy the journey!

Maria Swindell Gus
Executive Director
Bartlesville Convention and Visitor's Bureau

ACKNOWLEDGEMENTS

A big thanks (again) to my parents, who are now spirits on the other side themselves. But I still feel their presence every day.

Thanks to my many friends, who tirelessly listen to my ghost stories and who even ask about ghost stories for me when I am traveling with them. I love you guys, and you never tell me I am anything but just "so interesting" for wanting to know about the other side!

And an even bigger thanks to R.D., A.A., A.M., S.L.G., L.H., S.R., M.M., S.L. and E.K.W. for always cheering me on: you are my best friends. You keep my curiosity burning and love me anyway.

Last, thanks to Maria Swindell Gus of the Bartlesville Convention and Visitor's Bureau, who always patiently helped and answered my questions during the course of my writing this book.

INTRODUCTION

Let me just tell you from the get-go that I am a big believer in ghosts. If you have read my other two haunted books in this series, then you know I believe in and love ghosts. They exist, they are real and they are a part of the reality that we live in every day.

I personally believe in ghosts because the home I grew up in was haunted. It was (and still is) just an unobtrusive house that was built in the 1950s in Dallas, but it had so many ghosts while I was growing up that the house always felt extremely overcrowded. I also used to see the spirits out of the corner of my eye. I never knew what it was really, but I know I saw a movement, and there was a certain unexplained energy that was always present. When you're a kid, you don't really think about it, but nevertheless the ghosts were happy to be there.

I have never been able to actually see ghosts in their ethereal form (no, I am not the ghost whisperer and you'll likely not find too many people who are). I may have seen a ghost or two, but other than that, any sighting has been out of the corner of my eye.

However, I can feel them.

Let it be understood, too, that if you do go to the locations listed in this book searching for ghosts and find none, seeing a ghost may not be your talent. But keep your feelings, ears and even your nose open—subtle

Bartlesville, Oklahoma.

changes will let you know what's going on around you. And remember, we aren't all living in a television drama like *The Ghost Whisperer*. It really isn't as easy as the show makes it look, at least not for most people.

Regarding my house, I will say that I think the ghosts left with my mother when she died several years ago. Even though she was a true God-fearing woman, she was also a true ghost magnet and a believer in ghosts. Now that my brother lives in the house, I haven't felt a thing; he is not a ghost magnet, and I'm not sure he even believes in ghosts at all.

There are also two stories that convince me that ghosts do exist and that they live among us, which is one of the reasons I decided to write this book. While in my twenties, I moved away from Dallas to Chicago and then to Los Angeles. I didn't come back for twenty years, but during the time I was gone, my mom would always call me and tell me stories about the ghosts that were bumping around in my old home. (She and my dad stayed in that large house in Dallas until they both died.) Once, my mom called me up and said she had seen smoke coming out of her trash can in the bedroom. She smoked, and she said she thought she had accidentally put a lit cigarette in the trash can and that it had sparked a fire. However, she looked inside the trash can and couldn't find anything on fire. She went back to her business, and a few moments later, she saw the white filmy smoke coming out of the trash can again. She knew what it was this time, and she called me to tell me about it.

I suggested that she call a parapsychologist who could tell her what she needed to do to get rid of all these ghosts in her house. She thought about it and said she would call. The next day, she called and told me that she had spoken with a parapsychologist, and the woman told her what she needed to do in order to get rid of the ghosts. My mom said simply, "You know, they're not hurting anybody. I think I'll just keep 'em."

That was my mom.

By the way, if you do need to get rid of a ghost, the best thing to do is send it to the light; it might be a lost spirit that hasn't crossed over, and you sending it on its way could be one of the most generous things you will ever do.

Another time, I brought a friend of mine with me on a trip to see my parents at my old childhood home (it was the holidays), and we took some photos. My friend and I had just bought a digital camera and had not heard about the orb phenomenon yet. We were taking photos, and in almost all of the photos of my mother, there are orbs surrounding her. It was eerie. I have never taken photos of that many orbs again in my life, but my husband, who is a photographer, took quite a few images in my childhood home before my mom died, and you could always bet there were one or two orbs hanging around her.

One more story about my house, which by the way is not listed in any of my haunted books, as my brother lives there now and he would kill me. In high school, I had a best friend whose father would drop her off in the mornings around 5:00 a.m., and she would ride to school with me. She would often bring her laundry to do at my house in the morning, and in order to get to the laundry room, you had to go downstairs and take either a left through the living room and kitchen or a right down the hall into the den and kitchen and then, from either direction, proceed into our game room to the laundry room. One morning, she went downstairs, and about five minutes later, she came running back up into my room, looking like she had seen a ghost. She said she had. She said she heard this really loud breathing and felt something looking at her in the living room. That story still gives me chills when I think of it.

My mom did tell me when I was older that someone had died in that house. I never found out which room. I am still convinced the good spirits were my mom's friends (she had seen a lot of death during her lifetime) and that they were looking out for her family: me, my sisters and brother and, to a point, my dad, who never believed in ghosts or ever saw one (that he would admit to, anyway; he would have told it to go away if he had, and that would have been that).

I do believe there is a difference between ghosts and spirits too. Let me explain.

I have read many books on ghosts and spirits in my life and have come to the conclusion that there is a difference between the two. Although it all boils down to the same thing, I believe spirits come and go and are there when we need them, like ghosts, but that they are the souls of those we have loved and lost.

With ghosts, it seems they are more like entities who don't want to leave a place for whatever reason, or maybe a soul who does not know that he or she is even dead. There are also those instances when you hear of ghosts that keep repeating the same actions over and over again, just like they did when they were alive. These are what I call memory traces of events that have happened, and some people are in tune enough to be able to experience them.

Finally, my husband and I were in Belfast a few years ago. We visited the location where the *Titanic* was built (it's a huge hole in the dock area). I was talking with our guide while my husband was shooting photos. When we got home, he began looking at the photos he had taken and found one that he had shot of the dry dock. It was a photo of a man just standing by the dock. Not only was no one there that day, but there was also no way anyone could get down there. The man in the photo is wearing a yellow rain slicker, and it reminded me of a picture I once saw of the captain of the *Titanic* before it sank. The proof in this photo is there: someone showed up in that picture that day (and that picture only), either accidentally or on purpose.

When you go into a room or enter a place that feels a little unusual, pay attention to your thoughts and feelings and perhaps just say hello to a spirit that has come to see you.

One last story about a recent experience I had. A good friend of mine named John Macy from Los Angeles died, along my cousin, Egan Trammel, and my dad. After they all died, I felt that all three were watching over me on a regular basis. I always felt them on my left side, and I called them my three wise men. They were with me until a few years later when my mom died, and then I felt like she sort of took over the charge of "watching out for Rita Jo," and my three wise men were relieved of their duties. I still feel them sometimes, but not as often, and it always makes me feel so happy to know they have come to say hello.

And now, without further adieu, what you have been waiting for: a little history of the what, where and why of Bartlesville, Oklahoma, as told by Kay Little, education coordinator at the Bartlesville Area History Museum.

HISTORICAL AND HAUNTED BARTLESVILLE

On November 16, 1907, Oklahoma became a state. Ernest Lewis was an operator of a tavern that was located at the corner of Third and Keeler Streets and had been told by the U.S. deputy marshal, Fred Keeler, that as of Statehood Day, he could no longer sell hard liquor. Keeler and his deputy marshal, George Williams, showed up at the joint on Statehood Day, and Lewis shot at both of them, killing Williams. Keeler then killed Lewis. It has been said that Keeler and Lewis hated each other, and Lewis felt that Keeler had it in for him. Lewis's wife, Julia, was so mad that she wanted the headstone to read "murdered by Fred Keeler." The Keeler family didn't like that, and Julia decided on "killed by Fred Keeler." The headstone is still there at the White Rose Cemetery. This happened at 9:00 p.m., and it was the first shootout in the state of Oklahoma.

Back in 1870, when northeast Oklahoma was home to the Osage, Cherokee and Delaware Indians, an Indian trader named Nelson Carr opened a trading post on the north side of the Caney River.

And so began the legend of Bartlesville.

In 1875, Jacob Bartles, a Civil War veteran who saw an opportunity in Indian Territory, bought the mill from Carr and expanded the facility into a flour mill and eventually made it into a general store and home for his family. Bartles was married to Delaware Indian Chief Charles Journeycake's daughter, Nannie Journeycake Pratt. The marriage allowed Bartles to be a business owner in Indian Territory.

William Johnstone and George Keeler also came to the area in the early 1870s. Both gentlemen took Delaware Indian brides. After working for the Bartleses, the two struck out on their own and built a general store on the south side of the river. Within a few years, the area around the Johnstone-Keeler store had grown to include other businesses and dwellings. The population grew to nearly two hundred as settlers moved to the area. Bridges and railroads came to town, along with merchants, a drugstore and a school. In 1897, Bartlesville was incorporated, taking the name from its early settler and businessman.

Haunted places abound in Bartlesville.

The city expanded southward, past the Caney River, and Bartles was disappointed by his failure to secure the railroad station on the north side of the river. He moved his store three miles north to what is present-day

Dewey, named after Admiral George Dewey, who is well known today for his victory at Manila Bay.

Then the boom happened. It was Keeler who found another key to Bartlesville's future—oil. Keeler had noticed rainbow sheens on the area creeks and believed that there was an untapped oil supply beneath the Caney Basin. Keeler was right. On April 15, 1897, the first commercial oil well in what is now the state of Oklahoma—the Nellie Johnstone No. 1—blew in as a gusher. Nellie Johnstone was the Delaware maiden who owned the land where the well was discovered.

Attracted by the oil boom, Frank and L.E. Phillips, two brothers who were raised on an Iowa farm, came to Bartlesville in 1904. They hit a gusher just north of Bartlesville, followed by eighty straight producers. The two founded Phillips Petroleum Company in 1917. The company grew to become Bartlesville's largest employer and one of the nation's top oil companies.

Armais Arutunoff, a Russian immigrant, was another Bartlesville pioneer. At the urging of the Phillips brothers, Arutunoff came to the community with his invention—an electric pump that pumped oil from deep in the ground (this prototype would later become the REDA pump).

Today, Bartlesville is proud of the many attractions and assets that continue the legend of exploration and innovation, including museums, dramatic architecture, art collections, scenic prairie life and world-renowned events. It has grown and is now the home of more than thirty-four thousand people, as well as that of industrial giants ConocoPhillips, Schlumberger REDA Production Systems and Zinc Corporation of America. Since its early days, Bartlesville's business has been primarily in natural gas, oil, agriculture and ranching.

The sights and sounds of the city are important, too, and each year, citizens and visitors enjoy the diversity and entertainment of the Bartlesville Symphony Orchestra, Civic Ballet, Choral Society, Community Concert Association, Theater Bartlesville and Children's Musical Theatre.

Bartlesville is no stranger to music. Its annual OK MOZART Festival brings internationally recognized musicians and artists to the area every year, along with spectators and media attention.

For a dozen years, the National Biplane Association has selected Bartlesville for its Biplane Expo, and the SunFest Arts and Crafts Festival draws thousands of people to Sooner Park for family-oriented exhibits, music and arts and crafts every year.

Since its early days in Indian Territory, Bartlesville's history has been told through its architecture. The Dewey Hotel, a Victorian structure built in 1900, was the first frame building in Dewey. The Frank Phillips Home, the twenty-six-room mansion built by Bartlesville pioneer Frank Phillips in 1909, still houses the family's original furnishings and art collections. The beautiful La Quinta Foster Mansion, built in 1932 with terra cotta floors and hand-painted ceilings, is now part of Oklahoma Wesleyan University, a four-year liberal arts university with students from all across the world.

Area museums include the Price Tower Arts Center, the Tom Mix Museum, the Bartlesville Area History Museum and the museum at Woolaroc, the former country retreat of Frank Phillips. The Price Tower, which was completed in 1956, was designed and constructed by noted architect Frank Lloyd Wright for the H.C. Price International Pipeline Company. The tower now houses the Price Tower Arts Center and the Inn at Price Tower, a twenty-one-room boutique inn that offers upscale dining at its Copper Bar.

Woolaroc is one of the area's top attractions, boasting a 3,700-acre wildlife preserve, one of American's finest museums, the Native American Heritage Center, nature trails and the historic Frank Phillips Lodge. Area visitors can see exhibits on art, architecture, history and science at the Price Tower Arts Center. An architectural wonder is the Bartlesville Community Center, which was designed by the Frank Lloyd Wright Foundation. Other attractions in the area include the frontier town museum at Prairie Song, Indian Territory, the Keepsake Candle Factory and Country Store, Red Dirt Soap Company and the beautiful eleven-mile jogging and biking trail throughout the city known as Pathfinder Parkway.

The city of Bartlesville, as aforementioned, is named after Jacob Bartles, who bought a flour mill on the nearby north bank of the Caney River in

1875. At that time, much of the land in Bartlesville and nearby Dewey was simply being used for wheat fields.

Jacob Bartles was actually born in New Jersey and moved to Kansas when he was fifteen years old. When he married Nannie Journeycake Pratt, she was already widowed. The couple settled at what used to be Silver Lake in 1873, and then Bartles moved farther north in 1875 to start a trading post on Turkey Creek in present-day Bartlesville. On May 6, 1879, he established the first Bartlesville, Indian Territory post office, and today, there is a marker there that is several yards east of the present-day Dollar General store.

It should be noted that it was not Bartles but two of his former employees who turned the wheat fields along the Caney River into a town. In 1894, William Johnstone and George Keeler, who had both worked as clerks in the general store that Bartles owned, opened their own store on the south side of the Caney, and from there, business took off. Keeler was a good shopkeeper, and he also spoke fluent Osage. The store became a hit for the local Indian tribes in the area, and soon, the area itself became a town.

The first commercial oil well in Oklahoma, the previously mentioned Nellie Johnstone No. 1, was drilled by Johnstone, Keeler and a man named Michael Cudahy across the river from Bartles's mill. It blew in on March 25, 1897, and was "completed" on April 15.

In 1898, Jacob Bartles and a man named Colonel Porter began building a railroad grade that ran south from Caney, Kansas, and west of Bartlesville in the direction of the Collins coal mine in present-day Collinsville. Around this time, Bartles decided to move and start a new town, so he placed his store on log rollers and moved it overland, heading northeast along the railroad grade, all the while continuing to do business. He then started the new town of Dewey four miles from Bartlesville.

Bartlesville is located in the state of Oklahoma in both Osage and Washington Counties. It is about forty-seven miles north of Tulsa and closely borders Kansas. The city really had its heyday in the early 1900s with the development of the huge oil fields on the nearby Osage Indian Reservation. The oil fields around Bartlesville actually were not fully taken advantage of by the Department of the Interior until around 1905,

Downtown Bartlesville.

when oil leasing began. By 1907, things had taken off in Bartlesville in a big way, and the Santa Fe Railroad built a depot in Bartlesville in 1909. Passenger train service stopped in 1971, however, and Phillips Petroleum bought the depot in 1983 and remodeled it. The company donated it to the chamber of commerce in 1998.

While there are many myths and legends surrounding Bartlesville and its oil, it was a common fact that well-known resident Frank Phillips of Phillips Petroleum fame really did hold parties for former outlaws and lawmen in this area. He definitely used it to his advantage, too.

One incident happened on June 14, 1903, and it is hailed as the "most spectacular robbery in Oklahoma history" today. Outlaws Sam and Will Martin held up more than seventy-five people who were traveling on what was called the Old Road to Pawhuska on a Sunday afternoon, three miles west of Bartlesville on Liza Creek. Phillips happened to be traveling the Old Road, but the Martin brothers didn't disturb him. Phillips never had to worry about outlaws robbing him since they would only be hurting themselves. He was right, as in most of the choices he made after coming to Bartlesville, Oklahoma. And the rest, as they say, is history, some of which still hangs on in this Oklahoma town of legend and myth.

I

Restaurants and Bars

There are a number of restaurants and bars in Bartlesville, Oklahoma, but only one restaurant and bar really stood out with stories of hauntings from bygone eras. After all, it sits on a corner, and if this building could talk, what stories it would tell! And who can resist eating at a restaurant that was once a brothel, or having a drink next to an empty bar stool that might not be empty? One thing is for sure, you can be certain there are many stories to be told by the locals if you take the time to listen.

Restaurants and bars prove fun can be had in various parts of this city.

FRANK AND LOLA'S

200 East Second Street

I had been told that Frank and Lola's, which is located in what was formerly known as the Buford & Sons building, was haunted by a prostitute who worked in the basement during a bygone era. I had to find out the truth for myself.

The place is certainly unassuming enough, and the owners are friendly and don't mind sitting down to tell a ghost story or two if you take the time to ask. Even if you aren't planning on doing any ghost hunting, Frank and Lola's is still one of the best places in town to have dinner. The restaurant has an award-winning homemade salsa that is served with a bowl of fresh cooked tortilla chips, and it also has other menu items: green chili cheese fries; crispy flash-fried calamari tossed in a sweet Thai chili sauce; pulled pork; farm-raised catfish; and red beans and rice served side by side with pan-roasted andouille sausage.

My mouth was watering before I could even think about looking for the prostitute in the basement who, by the way, is reportedly named Estelle.

One story I heard about the ghost at this restaurant was from a woman who played the ghost herself during the filming of a Discover Oklahoma state tourism television show. The crew was filming tourist spots at the time, and they decided to add Frank and Lola's restaurant. The crew got all their needed footage at the restaurant and then went elsewhere to do more filming. When they got back to their office in Oklahoma City, all of the footage from Frank and Lola's was gone; it had literally disappeared. There was nothing but fuzz on the recording, though everything else was there. The crew then returned to Frank and Lola's to reshoot the restaurant, and from there, all was fine. However, after hearing the story, folks began to believe that Estelle was playing tricks.

Outlaws once frequented the building where the restaurant is now located, back in the days when it was a brothel. It was a convenient location since the Kansas state line is not far from Bartlesville, and most outlaws headed for the border when they needed to escape the law. In fact, it is a known fact that lots of different robbers and thieves hung out in Bartlesville, and there are many outlaw legends that take place in the downtown area, including one that says Bonnie and Clyde spent some time at a downtown hotel. It has also been rumored that Belle Starr hid out in the area.

According to one of the restaurant's owners, when they bought the building in the 1980s, there were still stalls with mattresses in the basement where prostitutes most likely slept. In regard to the ghost, the story goes that there was a prostitute downstairs who murdered one of her customers. No one knows why she killed him, but one can only imagine. Such a thing was not written about back then, but many old-timers swore that it happened, and locals now believe she is the restaurant's current ghost.

One night, while the restaurant was being filmed, there were some men working on the building, and the bathroom door started banging for no reason. On a different night, the owners left, locked the building and came in the next morning to find that the television was on and that the same bathroom where the banging had been heard previously

The inside of Frank and Lola's restaurant.

had paper towels thrown all over the floor. On another morning, the owner-chef came in and saw something out of the corner of his eye. He thought he saw someone, but when he turned around, there was no one there.

The bartender at Frank and Lola's also believes there is a ghost. He said that he was standing in the kitchen one day in the same spot where the owner had been standing when he saw the apparition. The bartender also saw someone, but when he turned to look again, the apparition was gone. It seems that the ghost only presents herself to men. There are no reports that she has shown herself to any women.

I walked down to the basement with local ghost hunter Scott Hickcock, and he said that he felt there was something down there that was curious. He also said that he felt a lot of despair and that something down there was constantly observing things.

Jared Hicks, a cook at the restaurant who is quite young and doesn't look like someone prone to making up ghost stories, said he has had two "pretty crazy experiences" himself. One was in the back room where the pool table is located. He opened the door to get some ingredients out of the back refrigerator, and before he could shut the refrigerator door, the entry door to the back room slammed shut. Jared said he freaked out a little bit and ran back up to see who it was, but there was no one there.

Jared also had another story to share. Every Monday, the restaurant gets its food inventory. One Monday, while he was putting away a load of food, he thought he heard a delivery guy in the kitchen. When he turned around, he saw that it wasn't a delivery guy but a "lady with a cigarette." All he could see, however, was the smoke coming out of the cigarette's end and a shadowy figure. Then all of a sudden, it was gone.

"This was about a year ago when I saw the figure and about the same time when the door incident happened," Jared said. What's even more interesting is that he still works there.

THE SOLO CLUB

408 East Second Street

Photographer Russell Dandridge and I were told to head to the Solo Club in Bartlesville and have a drink or two after our long day of looking for Bartlesville ghosts. Ghost hunter Scott Hickcock was with us, and he immediately picked up some interesting vibes as we walked in the door.

Before sitting down for a cranberry and vodka though, I looked around the dark bar and started asking the employees and patrons questions. One person who was a former employee told me she experienced two ghostly encounters while working at the club. One occurred at about 3:00 a.m. one night, when she was turning off all the lights. She looked around, and there was someone standing at the end of the bar. When

The Solo Club is good for a drink and a ghost story.

she turned back to take a second look, there was no one there, but then a cold wind blew through the place. The bartender described it as kind of creepy. She also said that her camera would sometimes turn off and on for no reason. But the most interesting story she told me was of an ice bucket flying through the air, as if someone had thrown it. The bucket actually flew out and around a corner before landing on the floor.

A regular at the bar added that he has never seen a ghost in his life, but he said that stories abound of ghosts at the Solo Club. He also added that he has heard people say that if you sit on a certain chair at the bar, you will soon die. "They all die because they sit right there," he said, pointing. Because of that, patrons at the Solo Club call the area where the chair is located the ghost corner. After the patron shared his story with us, Hickcock said that he sensed a tired energy and a feeling of weakness in the bar.

Another patron at the Solo Club had a ghost story to tell about an old nursing home called Heritage Villa, which is located on Highway 75. She said she had heard stories that right before a person passes away at the nursing home, they hear little children laughing and skipping down the hallway. When an employee goes to investigate, there are, of course, no children to be found.

II

DOWNTOWN BARTLESVILLE

Downtown Bartlesville was a happening place in its day, and actually, it still is, with shops, restaurants and a plethora of history on every corner. There are a number of ghostly legends in the downtown area and probably even more than we uncovered that are still left to be found.

Downtown Bartlesville has seen a lot of action over the years.

SWEET P'S

109 Southeast Frank Phillips Boulevard

According to Maria at the Bartlesville Convention and Visitor's Bureau, ghost hunters have explored Sweet P's and walked away with some great stories to tell.

Sweet P's is a cute little shop that sells all kinds of knickknacks, clothes and jewelry. The building in which Sweet P's is housed was once a law office and also a bank; in fact, it was the first bank in town and was opened by Frank Phillips.

As I headed up the back stairs of the shop to get some ghostly impressions, I was told the place had also once been a drugstore and a jeweler's shop. The employee I talked to at the store said ghost hunters had visited the building before and usually walked away with impressions that she felt came from the time when the building was a jewelry store. Scott Hickcock said he felt like he had been whacked on the head, and when we went upstairs, he said he felt as if he had walked into a bunch of cobwebs.

Sweet P's.

A man by the name of Mr. Derryberry owned the jewelry shop for a long time, and he also had a clock and watch repair business there, too. Hickcock wanted to know during the middle of the investigation if the man had been balding, as he was picking up the impression of a balding man. Mr. Derryberry was also a poet, and he would sell his poetry books at the store. Overall, it was agreed that if something was haunting the place, it would have to be Mr. Derryberry since he spent so much time at the store that he loved.

KNIGHTSBRIDGE BUILDING

122 Southwest Frank Phillips Boulevard

The Knightsbridge Building in downtown Bartlesville was the location of the first murder in Oklahoma, the murder that took place on Statehood Day. Teri Dearman, an employee of the company currently housed in the building, met with me to tell me a little about the building's ghost stories.

The basic story is that there was a bar downstairs, and Ernest Lewis was the proprietor. The bar served a homemade beer called a 2 percent beer. On Statehood Day, one eyewitness reported seeing one person come in the front door and one in the back where the beer was being illegally sold. Other reports described beer being sold to the Native Americans in the area, which was also illegal.

According to Dearman, a man named Williams walked into the bar and started shooting. As soon as he fired, someone else reportedly walked in through the back door. Williams then pushed the bartender down and said there was going to be some shooting. Lewis then pulled a gun and started shooting at Williams. Williams missed, and then the second man shot Williams. He then went through the front door and shot Lewis, and still today, records say that Ernest Lewis murdered Williams and that another man (supposedly named Keeler) killed Ernest Lewis in self-defense. But outlaws in the area believed that Lewis was actually murdered. Whatever the case may be, before the state had statehood, there was a time when there was no state official law enforcement but rather a special group of deputies who were in charge.

A corridor of the Knightsbridge Building.

Is there a ghost behind this door?

There has reportedly always been a lot of contention and drama in the spot where the Knightsbridge Building is now. The building housed three different hotels over the years, all of which were said to have been full of wild folk: the Utopia (1914), the Grand (1927) and the Oxford (1940–50). According to Dearman, the building became more respectable in later years, but for the most part, it had a reputation, for the street it was on was lined with brothels and "everything was all men and women with loose morals."

These days, employees in the Knightsbridge Building report hearing weird noises all the time, and those who have been in the building at night by themselves have reported hearing footsteps and things moving around. While Dearman said that she has never seen anything or felt anything evil, she does hear things all the time. She usually just turns up her radio and ignores it. The building's previous owners also claimed to have heard people walking. The layout of the building has not, for the most part, changed over the years.

Scott Hickcock said that while visiting the building, he felt something inside it, as if a person with a particularly strong emotion could not leave the building, perhaps because he or she was trapped. Scott also shared his thoughts on ghosts versus spirits while at this building. "A spirit is someone who crosses over and comes back," he said. "And a ghost is somebody who doesn't realize he or she is dead and gets stuck here. Sometimes you will get an intelligent kind."

On a tour of another part of the building, Scott was able to pick up orbs on his camera, and we both came away believing that something is definitely still there.

THE OLD COURTHOUSE

400 Frank Phillips Boulevard

The old courthouse in Bartlesville, Oklahoma, was built in 1913 by architect P.H. Weathers. Before it was a county courthouse, the building served as the old Bartlesville Post Office and as a federal courthouse. It was also listed on the National Register of Historic Places in 1981.

The old courthouse has great stories. Maria from the Bartlesville Convention and Visitor's Bureau shared a story with me about a woman she knew who had worked there for twenty-five years. The woman, Jane Ann Byrd, said that she always felt that there was a presence in the courthouse attic, and she often had to go up there to file papers. She said that the ghost up there never scared her since it was always very playful. It would turn the lights on and off and open and close the doors, just to let her know that it was there.

The owners eventually had all of the air conditioning and ductwork in the courthouse redone, and workers spent a lot of time in the attic. One day, the lead guy on the job walked by Jane Ann with a cigarette in his mouth, and she said that he was totally white and looked as if he were freaked out. She could tell there was something wrong, so she went after him and asked him if he was okay since she was the liaison between the people in the building and the workers. According to Jane Ann, the

The courthouse in Bartlesville.

man was definitely troubled. He began to explain the situation to her. Every night when he left the building, he put his tools away, and when he returned, they were always out of place. He figured since he had a lot of guys who worked for him that it was one of them playing a joke, so he never brought it up. He explained that the night before, he had deliberately put his tools away, shut the box and made sure he was the last one to leave because he was going to catch the guy who was playing with his tools. He was the last one to leave and the first one to get there for the job the next day. When he reached the attic the next morning, all of his tools were laid out.

That was enough to spook and bother him, but later, as he was working on a ladder, he looked down and saw a man—an apparition—dressed in clothes from a different era, standing between him and one of his men. The worker said he could see right through the man.

It was at that point that the worker said, "Forget this, I am done with this," and he took the ladder and stormed out of the building, completely spooked.

For Jane Ann, the worker's story validated all the things that she had experienced while she was working in the courthouse. One day, while she was downstairs in the basement, a place that at one time or another had served as the town jail, she started talking with one of the workers and began to complain about the ghost in the attic. Another worker who was down there sort of scoffed at Jane Ann's tale and said, "That's nothing." Apparently, someone worked every night in the basement monitoring the security cameras. The guard had seen a woman getting on and off the elevators, and the elevator doors were always opening and closing and going up and down when there was no one else in the building.

Another nearby courthouse that is said to be haunted is the Nowata Courthouse, which is in nearby Nowata where Jane Ann lives. According to Maria, Jane Ann often took papers back and forth between the courthouses. She says there used to be a bell in the Nowata Courthouse that dinged when someone opened the door, but it had been removed some time ago. There was a woman who was there late one night, and Jane Ann had gone there to deliver some papers. According to the story, they needed to go to another part of the courthouse. Jane Ann said she was already kind of spooked, but she went with the other woman. They both heard the bell at the door ding, despite the fact it had been removed years ago.

Jane Ann also said that when she was a deputy, she oftentimes saw lights at the old Memorial Hospital that had been turned on, and she would call over there and ask why the lights were on if the building was vacant. No one could ever explain that either.

HOPESTONE STUDIO

120 Southwest Frank Phillips Boulevard

Hopestone Studio is located in downtown Bartlesville and is also connected to the nearby restaurant Frank and Lola's and Knightsbridge Building. Maybe the ghosts move around back and forth from one place to the other without realizing they are entering other stores and buildings.

Whatever the case, Hopestone Studio is a gallery with one-of-a-kind art, pottery, jewelry, scarves, handbags and photography. One employee there said she was in the gallery by herself one night and heard very light footsteps. She also said that sometimes, when she is working by herself, she can hear the toilet flush.

"Ghosts don't like me, and I am not scared," she added.

Back in the 1930s and '40s, the building had been a grocery store, and later, it was an appliance store that mostly sold stoves and refrigerators. After the building stood vacant for a while, the current owner decided that she wanted a place downtown, so she bought the store and renovated it. She has never had any trouble. The employee added that the owner has never said anything about ghosts, so the employee has never brought it up.

III

CEMETERIES

Let's face it: no matter how many cemeteries a person visits during his or her lifetime, most people feel that graveyards are just a little creepy. As for me, I am always struck with a silent and peaceful sense of awe when I visit older cemeteries, like the one I discovered in Bartlesville

White Rose Cemetery.

Grave of John Winn, one of the older graves at White Rose Cemetery.

called White Rose Cemetery. A lot of history can be found here. I often wonder why a person would want to haunt a place where they are buried; one would think there would be more interesting places to relive one's life after death.

A psychic once told me that the dead may not realize that they are indeed dead and that they remain near their bodies trying to figure out what happened. One can only wonder.

WHITE ROSE CEMETERY

804 West Eleventh Street and Virginia Avenue

I talked with Kim Inman, the cemetery director at the White Rose, and she said that the White Rose is the oldest cemetery in the state of Oklahoma.

It is also the burial place of a man who was killed in a shootout during the first murder in Oklahoma.

The cemetery was established in 1899, and at the time, it was located outside of town. However, it wasn't as far away for some folks who lived near the town limits. Others kept burial plots on their land. Overall, however, the townspeople needed a cemetery that was closer.

At that time, the closest cemeteries were often hard to get to because the roads would flood with the rains or they were covered in snow during certain times of the year. The land originally belonged to the Cherokee Indians, but the town purchased the land from them in 1898. The first stone in White Rose Cemetery is dated 1893, which Inman said was interesting since the stone had been placed before the cemetery was even established. The plot belongs to Golda M. Hartman, a two-month-old who died on February 17, 1893.

The first recorded plot sold in the cemetery belonged to George Johnson in September 1906. Many of Bartlesville's more prominent people were buried at White Rose, and some people are entombed in

A few of the newer graves at White Rose Cemetery.

the mausoleum, which was built in 1923. Inman also said that bodies of some people who died before 1918 and who were buried in the cemetery were moved when the mausoleum was finished. It is the mausoleum that Inman said might be haunted.

Some of the people who are buried here died from interesting causes. The 1918 flu epidemic undoubtedly sent many to their graves. One story Inman shared was a heartbreaking tale of a woman who died of the flu shortly after her three sons.

"The obits were just. They have newspapers on microfilm [dating] back to 1895, and during that time, whole families were wiped out due to the flu," said Inman.

Inman also said that law enforcement back then rarely followed up on murders or death. She shared a story about two girls whose last name was Scroggins. "The newspaper account said that they killed themselves near the river by tying their hands behind their back and slitting their wrists," she said. "[According to the family], the older girl, who was sixteen years old, liked this boy, and the dad was against it, so they [the family] assumed

The cemetery's mausoleum.

that the girl went to the river, and her sister followed her, and they just died together and that was the account."

There is another burial in block six that belongs to a fifteen-year-old girl, and Inman thinks her last name was Baldwin and that she was kidnapped and taken across the state line. Around that time, the girl's family was feuding with another family, and there was a shooting. Eventually, the mother of the girl (who was pregnant at the time) was killed, along with the kidnapped girl's stepfather. The local paper published an entire account of the trial. Inman added that there are a slew of stories just like this one, so there's no telling which victim could be still be haunting White Rose.

As for the mausoleum, it is a fifteen-thousand-square-foot concrete building built in the Greek Neoclassic style and houses over five hundred crypts. It has a white stone exterior, a roof of vitrified tile and a white marble interior. The windows are made of ornamental leaded glass, and the doors and gates are made of bronze. The mausoleum was once privately owned by a man named Jim Bryant, who died in 1958 and was buried in the mausoleum with Masonic rites. He is buried next to his secretary.

White Rose Cemetery totals about twenty acres and holds over twelve thousand graves.

IV

HOMES

The most important homes in Bartlesville belonged to the town founders, one of whom was Frank Phillips. Even today, Phillips is regarded as one of the most important men in the city. So why wouldn't important Bartlesville founders want to hang around their old stomping grounds now and again just to make sure things are going as well as they would expect?

The lodge at Woolaroc Ranch.

THE FRANK PHILLIPS HOME

1107 Cherokee Avenue

While no one would fess up as to whether or not the Frank Phillips Home in Bartlesville is haunted, I feel that it might just be. While some say there are no ghosts there at all, one docent disagrees and says she definitely feels a presence.

Frank Phillips was an Oklahoma oil millionaire, and the Oklahoma Historical Society, which now maintains the home, offers tours through his pristine Neo-Classical–style mansion and a look at the life of one of America's most fascinating oil men back in the day.

Here's a little history about the home from the historical society's website: "Frank Phillips, an ambitious barber-turned-bond salesman from Iowa, visited Bartlesville in 1903 to assess business possibilities in the surrounding oil fields. He returned permanently two years later with his wife, Jane, and young son, John. After a series of failures that nearly caused him to abandon the business, a string of 81 straight successful oil wells ensured success." By 1909, Phillips had finished building the home. He lived there with his family until his death in 1950.

Phillips came to Bartlesville with his brother, Lee Eldas, and they drilled their first successful well in 1905. In 1917, the brothers founded the Phillips Petroleum Company, which eventually took over every aspect of the town. Phillips also built the Woolaroc Ranch in 1925 and the museum in 1929 (more on the ghosts there in the next chapter). Phillips Petroleum's world headquarters remained in Bartlesville until 2002, when it merged with Conoco. Today, the new ConocoPhillips company is headquartered in Houston, but Bartlesville is home to the company's Global Shared Services division, which includes the global information technology center, global financial services and human resources support organizations.

Phillips also has a street named after him, and the local hospital is named after his wife, Jane. The Frank Phillips Home, referred to as the "Grand Lady of Cherokee Avenue," has twenty-six rooms and has

The Frank Phillips Home.

been remodeled several times; the most recent remodel took place in the 1930s. Since that time, little remodeling has been done so visitors can get a good idea of what the home looked like back when it was a residence. Even the furniture and decorations have not changed. The home has a richly paneled library and a dining room where most of the family's entertaining took place. The Phillips family continually received guests at the house and also at Woolaroc Ranch.

Frank and Jane's bedrooms are on the second floor, along with their private bathrooms, both of which boast gold fixtures, Italian rose marble and ceiling mirrors. The walls of "Aunt Jane's bedroom," as Jane's room was called, are decorated with hand-carved wood and plaster. There is also a summer-sleeping porch that overlooks Cherokee Avenue where Jane could sit and watch her peacocks on the lawn. There is a barber's chair in Frank's bathroom, and he reportedly received a shave every morning from a local barber between 5:30 and 6:00 a.m. The walls of his bedroom are painted in a forest scene, and there are animal skins on the floor and across the couch.

There are also two other bedrooms on the second floor complete with stuffed animals and toys that belonged to the couple's foster daughters. There is an exhibit in the six-car garage behind the house, now called the Museum and Interpretive Center, that highlights the Phillipses' lives. The exhibit examines the family's beginnings, the history of the Phillips Petroleum Company and Frank's success and the philanthropic choices the family made during their lifetime through photographs and family artifacts. There is also a twenty-minute video on the history of oil in Oklahoma and the Phillips Petroleum Company. The Museum and Interpretive Center is where guests begin their tour.

Other things to take note of while looking around the house for ghosts are the mahogany woodwork, silk damask wall coverings, Waterford crystal chandeliers and exquisite oriental rugs. In the library, there are two thousand volumes of books ranging in subject from agriculture and military history to religion and children's stories.

The historical society's website also notes that between the years 1909 and 1917, the third floor was the private realm of John Phillips, the Phillipses' only natural child. After John left home to attend school, the third floor was used for various purposes. A room for the butler, Henry Einaga, was added during the 1930s remodel. Interestingly enough, Einaga secretly became a millionaire in the 1940s but continued to work for the family until his death in 1969 at the age of eighty-one.

While visitors to the Frank Phillips Home will have to determine for themselves if they feel any energy from the other side, the home is splendid. And really, who wouldn't want to come back and hang out there if given the chance?

THE FRANK PHILLIPS HOME AT WOOLAROC

1925 Woolaroc Ranch Road

www.woolaroc.org

Many docents at the Frank Phillips Home at Woolaroc claim that "Uncle Frank" still spends time at the lodge there. The ranch and retreat is about ten miles southwest of Bartlesville and is called Woolaroc, which is a combination of the words woods, lakes and rocks.

Today, the 3,700-acre ranch is still in operation and includes a museum exhibit of the Phillipses' extensive Native American, western and fine art collections and houses one of the most complete private collections of

Woolaroc.

Colt firearms in the world. The Phillips family lodge and mausoleum are also on the property, along with a huge wildlife preserve where visitors can see herds of American bison, elk, Texas longhorn cattle, water buffalo, zebra and more than twenty other animal species.

One particularly interesting incident that occurred at Woolaroc was the attempted kidnapping of Frank Phillips by "Pretty Boy" Floyd. Fortunately, Phillips had been told about the kidnapping plan by his friend, the outlaw Henry Wells. Apparently it paid for Phillips to have friends who were outlaws.

I brought Scott Hickcock with me on my second visit to Woolaroc. "The closer you get to night, the energy shifts," Hickcock said as we were leaving.

One woman who works at the reserve told me that she once had a conversation with someone who claimed that they had seen Frank Phillips walking around inside the lodge. The woman also reported hearing people walking around upstairs when no one was there.

The lodge was built in 1925, and Frank often brought investors there, as well as other guests. From American and foreign businessmen to local ranchers, cowboys and even Native Americans, all were welcomed at Woolaroc at one time or another. After he finished the lodge, he started construction for the museum. The first room, which was the airplane hangar, was completed in 1929. As his art collection grew, so did the building, and every decade or so, Frank would add a few more rooms.

The lodge's poker room is said to be haunted, and Frank would often bring a lot of his investors and friends there to play poker. According to one story, while playing poker with the owner of Ringling Brothers Circus, Frank put up one of his oil leases while the owner put up the rights to his circus. The owner, however, lost his hand, and Frank won the circus. They played cards again the next day. This time, however, Frank lost, and the owner won back his circus. A few months later, one of the circus's Asian elephants died, and the head of the elephant was presented to Frank as a gift. The elephant head is still hanging on the wall.

The chandeliers in the lodge came from the original Waldorf Astoria Hotel. Frank invested a little over $1 million in the hotel, so when it closed,

Many good times were had at the lodge, and some say Frank Phillips is still there.

he took the chandeliers in exchange for his money. The chandeliers have hung in the lodge ever since and are called "the million dollar chandeliers."

One of the docents told me that all of the photos on a wall in Jane's room were of guests whom Jane liked. However, if Jane decided she did not like someone anymore or if someone irritated her, she would take down that person's photo and replace it with someone else's.

I found that the daughters' bedroom felt the most haunted. Some say that something ghostly is going on in John's room, too.

The staff members at Woolaroc (at least the ones who will admit it) believe that Uncle Frank still hangs out at the lodge, and no one seems to mind either. It's also said that Frank wanted a phone put in the mausoleum where his body is now located. No one knows why; maybe just in case he needed it on the other side. The mausoleum itself is said to be quite beautiful as well. It is the kind of place that would not be so bad to hang out in for an extended period of time. Unfortunately, visitors are not allowed to visit there and see for themselves.

The poker room at Woolaroc.

Junior curator Shiloh Thurman says that there has been talk of ghosts haunting the museum. "They say there are occasionally folks who have said they have heard Frank walking down the steps," said Thurman, "and he used to tap his ring on the metal railings or walk in the halls from time to time."

Another docent also said that she heard the ring's echo and that it sounded heavy. But when she went to investigate, there was nothing there. This particular docent also said that the poker room is haunted and that there have been some docents in the lodge who have heard a sound, either the doorbell or the door opening. But instead of being afraid, they just say, "Hi, Frank."

THE MANCILL HOUSE

909 Southeast Cherokee Avenue

This house is also called the "Baroness House," but the owner's real name is Jana Majors, and she goes by "Baroness Ampersand." (She is also the owner of Baroness Ampersand Studio, which is sometimes called the Barony.) While it is a private residence, the home is located on the Cherokee Historical Walk, and Tulsa Ghost Investigators have paid a visit to the home to search for ghosts that may reside there.

The home was built in 1918 by Howard E. Mancill, and it has been occupied by fourteen families over the years, two of which were headed by Episcopal priests. The Middle European–style home is made of brick and wood and has two front doors. The home has changed little over the years; the screened-in back porch was converted into a breakfast nook in the 1970s, and a room upstairs was opened into the master bedroom.

When Tulsa Ghost Investigators visited the home, they were told that unexplained events often took place: loud knocking on doors, "heat shimmers," music that would play when the stereo was turned off and some unknown entity tripping people, to name a few. One family member even reported seeing a tall man with a beard on the staircase. The family living there also said that they continually feel as if they are being watched. Additionally, mist has been seen in the upper hallway, and the chandelier in the master bedroom is said to move on its own.

One of the most intense events at the Mancill House reportedly occurred about nine years ago at three o'clock in the morning. Jana Majors and her dog were alone in the house, and both heard someone enter using a key. The man made his way up the staircase and then quietly knocked on a door down the hallway from Jana's bedroom. Later, Jana learned that a man who used to live two blocks down the street returned to his former home drunk and let himself in with his old key. He was shot on the staircase by the new homeowner who thought he was a burglar and died instantly.

The Tulsa Ghost Investigators visited the house one August 13, 2004, a Friday. The investigators did not notice any apparent signs of paranormal

The Mancill House.

activity when they first arrived, but they did note that they could feel an energy on the staircase and in the upstairs hallway.

Later in the evening, they conducted a longer investigative session, turning off the power in the home and setting up their equipment to record. They recorded some knocks and pops, and visible points of light were seen on the staircase, as well as mist and dark shadows.

One of the investigators also noted that she felt the energy on the staircase was a child, and another investigator's watch had stopped during the investigation, but it started back up after the investigation was over.

The investigative team also recorded eight different sounds at the Mancill House, seven of which were male voices. In one of the recordings, you can hear someone saying the word "Ally." Pictures of orbs have also been taken on both digital film and on a 35mm camera, and there appears to be a vortex in the daughter's bedroom. The orbs have ranged over the years from groups of faces with beards and protruding lips to large, milky orbs with movement.

PRIVATE RESIDENCE AT HILLCREST

1848 Hillcrest Drive

While I was at the Hillcrest Country Club in Bartlesville investigating ghosts that may live there, a woman named Mindy approached me and told me about a ghost that lived in a house in town near where she grew up:

> *The home at 1848 Hillcrest Drive was built by my grandfather in about 1950. Where we lived was really more like a house. It is a two-story home that has four one-story apartments attached to the back of it. The whole complex was always called apartments though, even though I consider it a house and even today, these units are still considered apartments.*
>
> *After my grandfather moved out of the house, a family named Lyons lived there for a few years. Right after I was born in 1959, we moved into the apartments, too, and my parents lived there until about eight years ago when they bought the house they live in now.*
>
> [The] *upstairs was one very large room. At the end of the room was a very short hallway that led into the bathroom. On either side of the hallway were very tall closets. This hall wasn't more than maybe four feet long. The ghost that lives there seemed to reside in the hallway space. It didn't matter what the temperature was, that hallway always felt very cold. When my sister and I were young, we shared the upstairs room as our bedroom. I remember strange sounds coming from the small hallway when we would go to bed. It sounded as if the closet doors were being opened just slightly and then closed. I remember always wanting to have the light on outside the bedroom in the stairwell that went downstairs because being in the dark in that room was very creepy. I remember waking up in the middle of the night feeling like someone was watching me, and I would be afraid to roll over and look towards the small hallway where the closets were, so instead I would close my eyes very tightly and pray that whatever was in those closets wasn't going to come get me.*

My sister remembers feeling the same way. She always felt that something terrible happened in that area of the room at some point, but neither of us know what that would be or who would have been involved.

Overall, I have no idea who this ghost would be. No one died in that house to my knowledge. I know Mrs. Lyons died while they were living there, but my dad doesn't think she actually died in the house. I have often wondered what the grounds were like before my grandfather built the home. I know there were woods here, but I don't know if perhaps the land was also some sacred Indian ground or something since there are so many of those in Bartlesville.

Mindy also mentioned a few other haunted places in Bartlesville. When she was a kid, there was a boarded-up old house where a dentist named Dr. Born used to live. She said that he killed his wife there. The place was always cold, and it always sounded like someone was walking around upstairs, almost as if they were pacing back and forth. The house was torn down years ago.

"I am a strong believer in the supernatural and have had several experiences where I felt the presence of others," Mindy said. "I had what I truly believe was a ghost living in my house in Denver, too, since my soap would disappear all the time. Then one day before I was moving, I went up into the crawl space above my bathtub and there in the corner, stacked very neatly, were all my bars of soap. I guess it was a very clean ghost, but that's another story."

LABADIE MANSION

Copin, Oklahoma

Of all the places near Bartlesville that were mentioned to me, Labadie Mansion was the one place I was told about the most. The mansion has a lot of mystery and legend surrounding it, and after hearing various stories, I found that they were all connected.

In fact, this house seems to be the stuff that legends are made of for kids who are looking for a spooky story to tell.

These days, the house is in ruins, and it is a long walk up the hill it sits on to see what is left of it. According to the legend, Frank and Samantha Labadie (who was seven years younger than Frank) were wed in the 1880s. They lived with a man named Enos Parson, who was either a slave who did not wish to be freed after the Civil War or a hired handyman. The Labadies did not have any children, and when Samantha became pregnant, Frank knew it wasn't his and believed it was Parson's child. He waited until the baby was born to find out. Labadie killed Parson with a .44 Henry rifle and threw Parson's body into a creek. He later shot his wife and said at that time that he was being haunted by the ghost of Enos Parson. Not soon after, Frank shot himself.

As the story goes, on April 1, 1935, Frank took out his Colt House Pistol, shot Samantha four times until she was dead and then killed himself with one shot. When the bodies were found, the sixth bullet was missing from the gun. When the house was searched, the .44 Henry rifle that he supposedly used to kill Parson was never found. There is, however, no record of an Enos Parson in Bartlesville, and according to some of the locals, the Labadies died of smoke inhalation in a fire, not from a murder/suicide.

It is said that both the Labadies and Parson haunt the place. Whatever the case and whoever might be haunting the building, people who have gone up to the house have reported feeling that they were being watched and also a sense that they were uninvited. There are also reports that flashlights and other battery-operated equipment have stopped working while visitors were in the house. Some have said that they have heard phantom voices calling out names, and one paranormal investigator said that he smelled "burnt human flesh." People looking for ghosts in the mansion have also said that remnants left in the fireplace occasionally ignite on their own.

It is said that Frank's ghost can be aggressive toward anyone who enters what is left of the home. Enos Parson is also said to haunt the woods and the creek where his body was cast.

The home is a nineteenth-century Victorian mansion nestled among beautiful albeit twisted trees. According to the descendants of the Labadie family, none of these eerie ghost stories is true, and they insist that Frank and Samantha died in a fire that started when their gas heater malfunctioned. One thing is for certain though: both Frank's and Samantha's graves are located in the nearby cemetery, and there is no indication that a child or Enos Parson is also buried there.

GETTING THERE: From Bartlesville Municipal Airport, turn left onto CR-3007 South and then turn left again onto U.S.-60 East. Take another left onto U.S.-75 (Washington Boulevard) and then another left onto North 3970 Road. Turn left onto SR-10 (west) and keep left on West 900 Road. The name of the road changes to East 0090 Road. Keep right onto CR-3011 (northwest) and turn right (east) onto Local Road. You will see Labadie Cemetery. Turn west on Local Road and make a left (south) onto CR-3011. Turn right (west) onto Local Road. The remains of the mansion are about 0.3 miles down.

V

HOTELS

Who doesn't know a story about some haunted hotel somewhere or, at least, some great ghost story that involves a hotel? Bartlesville has its own haunted hotel story. And Dewey, the town next to Bartlesville, is actually famous for the haunted stories about its hotel. In fact, some believe the hotel is actually haunted by Jake Bartles, Bartlesville's namesake.

Are the hotels in Bartlesville haunted?

HOTEL PHILLIPS

821 South Johnstone Avenue

The Johnstone Apartment complex was once Hotel Phillips, and I have heard from a number of sources that ghosts (possibly former residents who have passed away) have indeed been seen at this location.

Maria from the Convention and Visitor's Bureau shared a story with me about the hotel and a girl named Tracy who used to work for her.

"Tracy was a pretty God-fearing woman and not open to all of this ghost stuff, but she said she definitely saw a light or orb in the basement, which is where Grill 66 is now," Maria explained.

A presence is also said to be on the seventh floor, and one of the employees reported that he once saw an orb on the surveillance camera.

The Hotel Phillips that once stood here is now an apartment building.

THE DEWEY HOTEL MUSEUM

801 North Delaware Street
Dewey, Oklahoma

Ghost hunters have explored the Dewey Hotel Museum and agree that it is haunted.

The Dewey Hotel Museum, located in historic downtown Dewey, Oklahoma, is a Victorian-style hotel that was built in 1899 by Jake Bartles, Bartlesville's namesake. The museum is furnished with period pieces and includes exhibits on Dewey's and Bartlesville's history, Bartles's family history and Indian women's art and craft collections.

The Dewey Hotel actually became the center of activity in the early days of oil development in the northern part of Washington County, and the Dewey Round-Up was established in 1908 from plans laid out in the Dewey Hotel. The Round-Up eventually became the biggest attraction ever launched in Washington County, drawing in crowds as large as twenty thousand to thirty thousand during the 1920s.

The Dewey Hotel Museum.

The Dewey Hotel is three stories tall, with large porches and cupolas above the roof. The old hotel has certainly earned a place in the history of Washington County, but some say there are guests who just can't leave. Some swear there are ghosts on the third floor.

In 2008, a ghost-hunting group came to the hotel

and recorded some footage for a DVD. While there, they said that they definitely felt there was a presence in the room called the King Bedroom. As it turns out, the King Bedroom was Jake Bartles's room when he was still alive, and it is possible he is still there. After all, he was the founder of Dewey and the man for whom Bartlesville is named.

The group also said they had felt a presence in a little theater down the street, and there have been several projectionists who have said that they, too, have felt a presence there over the years.

The ghosts could be anyone from the Dewey Round-Up crew. The Round-Up operated from 1908 to 1949. The Washington County Historical Society opened the hotel as a historical museum in 1967.

VI

More Hauntings

It really seems that Bartlesville is teeming with ghosts. Other spots rumored to be haunted include the old Santa Fe Depot; the Terrace Room, which is a part of ConocoPhillips; and quite a few private homes. As I drove up and down the streets of this beautiful city, I definitely felt a certain kind of energy that belonged to another place and time.

Another place rumored to have a few ghosts is Central Middle School on Southeast Ninth Street. While I couldn't get anyone to share any

Is Central Middle School haunted too?

specifics, the school was built in 1917 and was designed to house 450 students. Who or what haunts the school now is anyone's guess, but you should visit and see for yourself.

HILLCREST COUNTRY CLUB

1901 Price Road

I met with a man named Gordon Welch at the Hillcrest Country Club, and he immediately began to put me at ease with his ghost stories. When I walked away, I knew there was definitely something ghostly at this place.

Welch explained that the clubhouse was built in 1924 and was originally where the pool is today, but it burned down. The current clubhouse reopened in 1964.

The total cost of the building was one dollar in 1924, and it was purchased by the Phillips Drilling Company that same year. Welch can't remember if the company was Phillips Drilling or if it was a ConocoPhillips company. For many years, the Adams Building in downtown Bartlesville kept the original one dollar in the building's safe.

Another interesting thing about this country club is that there is a cemetery out in the middle of the golf course (the course was near the original clubhouse before it burned down). In fact, it is one of the only golf courses in the country with a cemetery in the middle of it. Welch worked at the Hillcrest Country Club from 1987 to 1990, and he has a story of an incident, one that he will never forget:

> *I was twenty-five, and I was in my office. It was December 1988, and we had a little man here, and he was probably sixty-five years old at that time. His job was to come in at 10:00 p.m. every night, lock the place up and vacuum and clean while everyone was gone. Then he would leave at around 5:00 a.m. and unlock when he left.*
>
> *The Christmas party had just finished and this man always started downstairs toward the men's locker room. He came up to my office* [and] *I looked at him, thinking* [he was] *physically shaken. He said to me,*

Hillcrest Country Club is one of a few golf courses in the United States with a cemetery.

> *"I have fought in World War II, I have played on the side of banks of rivers with dead bodies and I have seen it all, and there is nothing that scares me more than the war, but I can tell you just now that there was a man downstairs and I talked to him and he turned around and looked at me and then he was gone."*

The man told Welch he was not going back down there again. Welch said that was the beginning of this man's retirement.

Welch said that there was a man (he couldn't remember his name) who had a heart attack down there one day after he had finished playing golf. He died in the men's locker room. The cleaning man had, incidentally, known the man in life, and when he saw the ghost come out of the bathroom, the cleaning man had called him by name. When the ghost started to move away, the cleaning man yelled the name. The ghost then turned around to face the man and then disappeared.

Another grave at Hillcrest Country Club.

Some graves are old and some are new.

Welch did remember that the cleaning man was a strait-laced guy who did not drink or smoke.

Other things that have happened at the club over the years include the lights going on and off for no apparent reason. A paranormal society came a year and a half ago to investigate the club's grounds and cemetery.

The cemetery is actually an Indian cemetery; it belonged to the Delaware tribe before the tribe sold it to the county in the early 1900s. At that point, the county began using it for burials. A wooden fence once surrounded the cemetery, but Gordon said that he believes there are graves beyond the fence that sits on the course today.

There is also a man who lives in a house near the cemetery, and when he worked at the country club, he would not go near the cemetery, even during the day. There is a grassy area near the cemetery, and the man was grooming the green one night when he heard somebody whistling at him. The whistling sound came from the cemetery. He said nobody was there, but something kept whistling at him, and it scared him to death.

Even today, the cemetery does not have a name; it is just called Delaware Cemetery, after the Delaware tribe. If you are playing golf at Hillcrest, the cemetery is located near the sixteenth hole. While at Delaware Cemetery, I felt a sense of peace. It was as if I could feel the energy there, and while it was a good feeling, I'm certain that it could easily turn into a bad one. When I think about it, I do remember feeling as if I were being watched, but the eyes didn't feel evil.

BARTLESVILLE COMMUNITY CENTER

Adams Boulevard and Cherokee Avenue

Most ghost hunters and those who write ghost books can pretty much bet that there will be a ghost and a good ghost story at any local town theater. So it was with a real sense of excitement that I arrived at Bartlesville Community Center, the home of many of the city's stage productions.

The center was designed by Wesley Peters, chief architect of Taliesin Architects, and cost $13.5 million. It paid for itself on opening day. The interior's design features a lot of smooth curves and rounded lines, and the center also has a cloisonné mural of the northeastern Oklahoma countryside that is over twenty-five feet long. The meeting hall and foyer area also have crystalline light fixtures that hang from the ceiling like icicles, and there are also original paintings and sculptures on display in various locations.

The actual theater is located on the lower level and is known as the Studio Theatre. A functional balcony surrounds the front and side of the building, and some ghostly activity has also been felt up there. There is also the Marie Foster Performing Arts Hall, which is often referred to as one of the finest concert halls in the country. From national symphonies to Broadway and ballet, there is something for everyone at the Bartlesville Community Center—even something for ghost hunters.

I met with Bill Cheverton from the community center, and during the course of our conversation, he mentioned that the house he lives in is haunted. He has lived there for thirteen years, and he seems to have had

The community center hosts many theatrical productions during the year.

ghostly experiences all of his life. As for the ghosts at the theater, the main ghost (to the best of Cheverton's knowledge) was a schoolteacher who was forced to retire. She reportedly spent her last days on the playground watching over the children at the school where she taught. The playground sat close to where the stage is currently located.

The schoolteacher eventually passed away, and her ghost came back and watched over the children on the playground for many years after that.

Cheverton said that he didn't know the timeline for any of this other than the fact that Garfield Elementary, the school where the woman taught, was the first public school in Bartlesville. It opened in 1904, so the woman most likely taught sometime in the early 1900s. The school was eventually torn down, and because the woman's spirit had nowhere to go, she stayed on the school grounds, even after it became the community center.

Cheverton has been an employee of the theater for twelve years. He started in the fall of 1999, and after working there for six months, he became aware of the ghosts that haunted the center's theater. Cheverton said:

> *We were loading out a show* [a phrase that means taking down the stage and equipment], *and just as you can hear the stomping now, that was exactly what we were hearing and there was nobody there. We all heard it and turned around and looked and no one was there. A few minutes later, it happened again and about the third time it happened, the three of us split up because we figured there was somebody in the building. We all went in different directions and met back in the front lobby, and of course, there was no one else in the building except for us. So, we started realizing that there was a ghost here at that point and started doing some research and talking to other people, and of course, the stories go all the way back to when the community center first opened.*

The community center opened in 1982, and not long after, people reported seeing the ghost in the kitchen. A maintenance man who worked at the center several years ago also claimed that he spotted her on the stairwell and tried to chase her up the stairs and back down.

"It was one of those things where he was the only one in the building and no one else was here," said Cheverton. "I have never personally seen her, but I know she is there with me, and I feel her very strongly." Cheverton said that he often feels her presence when he stays late to finish up work. "She would come up there and just sit at the desk with me…She loves to play practical jokes."

According to Cheverton, the theater puts on a big production every year, and sometimes they use fog machines that create fog that is so thick, it's nearly impossible to see the other side of the stage. The machines have never set off a fire alarm. However, Cheverton said that during a production of *A Christmas Carol* one year, a little candle that was used during the show set off the fire alarm. Cheverton, however, thinks it was actually the ghost who set off the alarm.

"We also had a couple of experiences before the show when we were getting ready," said Cheverton. "For that show, we had been up on the grid, and [when we] came down off the grid, everything was secure. We walked across the stage and heard something hard hit next to us that had fallen from the grid, yet there was nothing there. We all three heard it as it came down, and it hit a couple of pipes and the floor right next to us. But there was nothing there."

Cheverton also said that when the show was over, they finished loading up and locked up the building, even double-checking the doors to make sure they were secure. But a few moments later, they found that one of the front doors wasn't latched, even though they had latched it.

"Two of us were working on that, and we heard a noise in the community hall. So we went to look in there, and it turns out that a security officer was having the same problem with the door up there. We spent about twenty minutes messing with these two doors. It was 2:00 a.m. and we were tired and we wanted to go home," Cheverton said.

"I said, 'To heck with it, I am going back stage and getting changed and then coming back up here and putting chains on the door and let someone else worry about it tomorrow.' So I went back and got the chains, and [when I came] back up, both of the doors were latched and that was after three of us had messed with them. There are tons of stories that I have like that."

According to Cheverton, the ghost, whom he calls Georgetta, also spends time in the auditorium. "When you look at our auditorium, there is just a whole sea of seats out there, and you can't tell if there is a chair down, but once again you will hear the coughing out there, and you know that she is out there pretty much all of the time whenever we are doing anything." He added that it was he who named her Georgetta, but he does not believe that is her real name.

> *After a couple of years, I got tired of just calling her "the ghost," so I named it George. At that point, I knew it was a schoolteacher, but I didn't know that it was a female, so it was just George. I called it George for several years, and one day, I walked into the front office and one of the ladies in the office said come to tell us about George, so I ended up standing in a big group up in the main hallway in the front lobby. There were about seven of us, and we are all talking about it* [the ghost]. *A woman, Pat Smith, who was the managing director at the time, asked, "Are y'all talking about the ghost?" She said that it wasn't a man but that it was a woman, and Pat knew a lot more about the history of* [the ghost] *than I knew at that point. I knew a lot more of the current stuff, so Pat filled in a lot of the holes as far as the history of the ghost. She said it was a female, so the name changed from George to Georgetta at that point.*

Georgetta is also said to hang out on the north side of the building, and the offices are on the south side. She goes over there occasionally. According to Cheverton, she was also there while I was interviewing him, listening to our conversation.

"I have been in other theaters, and there are ghosts," he said. "She is not the only one here, but she is the main ghost here. Actually, she is here with us right now."

Cheverton also shared an experience he had a few years ago. One night, while he was working late on a table saw, an Indian chief came in and watched over him. He said that was the first and only time he had ever seen the chief, and he did not realize at the time who he was. "I just knew someone was watching over me, and in the next fifteen or twenty minutes, it became clear to me that this gentleman was an Indian chief."

Who is the ghost who haunts the auditorium here?

Cheverton had one last bizarre experience to share with me:

> *Like I said, she* [Georgetta] *used to come up and sit in my office. I was on my computer sometime around 3:00 a.m. and suddenly got this sensation. It started at the top of my head. People ask me if it was* [a] *cold* [sensation] *or if it was hot, and it was everything—I can't describe what the actual sensation was. It started in the tip of my head, and over a period of about twenty seconds, it moved all the way through my body, and I sat there and I was working on the computer and I realized after about two minutes that I could not look away or move away, but my hands would work. I had that sensation for two or three minutes, and it went from the tip of my toes right back up and right back out* [of] *the top of my head. She wanted to know what a computer was* [Georgetta was apparently an elderly woman when she died. Cheverton says he has never researched it, but that it just

> feels that way.], *and she got into me so she could see and experience what a computer was…*
>
> *There was a new employee here* [once], *and she was a photographer and loved taking pictures of storms, and there was a big storm blowing into Bartlesville one night. At about 11:00 p.m., she called me and asked, "Can I come down and take pictures?" and I said sure, just let me know when you are here and let me know when you leave. She came in and let me know she was here and then went up to the balcony. About fifteen or twenty minutes later, she showed up at my office* [and was] *white, asking, "Why were you doing that to me?"*
>
> *"Doing what?" I replied. "Why were you up there turning the lights on and off playing jokes on me?" And I told her that I had been sitting there the whole time and had not left my office. Once again, there were only two of us in the building, and she was on the balcony taking pictures, and there was* [a] *figure standing in the doorway that kept turning the lights on and off on her. The interesting thing is there is not a light switch up there—it is on the breaker panel downstairs. She could see whatever it was turning the switches.*

Shortly after that, all of the employees did a ghost walk through the building. Cheverton recounted a conversation they had on the way to the lighting booth. "I was telling them something about what goes on in the booth and one of them asked, 'Bill, why is it there are seven of us in the booth and everyone has a reflection in the glass except for you?' Not only did I not have a reflection in the glass, but the person who was standing directly behind me was in full view."

Before I left, Cheverton said that he believes there is a difference between a ghost and a spirit, and he thinks the hall is really half-full of spirits.

"There are times at night when I have heard hundreds of children's voices. You don't actually hear them—they are in your mind, but you know they are there," he said. "This is a place of excitement, and it is where kids love to come. Once again, we used to have the children's events in here, so there were children in here all year, and we used to also have children at the school's auditorium, and they did all their productions here. This place is full of spirits, and they love being here too."

Georgetta is said to wander around backstage at the community center.

THE BARTLESVILLE ARMORY

1816 West Hensley Street

Since Scott Hickcock was traveling with me, I asked him to take me to one of the places in town that he felt was especially haunted. He directed me to the armory and told me this story about his experiences while working there several years ago.

> *When I was recruiting down here at the armory for the army, they kept telling me that I would hear footsteps in the armory at night, and sure enough, I did. As a recruiter, I worked long hours and late nights making phone calls, sometimes until 9:00 p.m., and I would hear people inside the dang building. One night while I was working,* [I heard] *someone knock at my door. I opened the door and no one*

> *was there, and my recruiting officer that I chose was all the way at the end of the hall. I opened my door and looked down there, and I could have heard anyone leave, but there was no one there. And then I heard the showers turn on several times, and I would* [also] *hear the stalls slam, and the water* [from the sink] *would run on its own.*

Hickcock said that he also sensed that there were old soldiers in the building. He explained that these guys get attached; the guards get attached to the unit, so it is a feeling of old soldiers, and he felt those impressions very strongly.

"There was definitely a ghost, and it felt like someone that was lost, but nothing ever manifested itself to me," he explained. "I also felt like I was being watched, and I would shut my door at night, and sometimes when I would come back the next morning, my door would be open, even when I knew I had locked it."

The Bartlesville Armory.

He said other people who had worked at the armory had their own stories to tell, too, and added that the ghost's name is George.

"Being [the only one] here at night in the wintertime, it can get spooky even with no ghosts," he said. "It is an older building, and there has been a lot that has gone on in it for good or bad."

KEEPSAKE CANDLES

263 County Road 3022

Keepsake Candles in Bartlesville is located in an old air force base. According to the company's promotional material, each candle is handmade to customer specification, and the molds from the candles are taken from antique glassware dating from 1820 to around 1940. The molds for the store's original pottery are also from this time period. There is also a shop that sells the candles in addition to the back room where the candles are made.

In the fall of 1969, Alice Ririe, president of Keepsake Candles, decided to make crafts for an annual church bazaar in her kitchen. According to her husband, the project got a little out of hand. Fast-forward to the present, and Alice's project turned business is still going strong.

In 1975, the company moved its factory from County Road to its present location in the Osage Hills. The building was an air force radar base in the 1950s and '60s, so employees believe that the ghosts that haunt the candle factory are from that time. According to one of the stories I heard, an old lady was working in the base by herself one night and heard the men's urinal flush. Another lady who worked there reported seeing a man out of the corner of her eye while she was at the register. He was dressed in a military uniform, but when she looked in that direction, the man was gone.

There were about 250 people stationed at the base at one time, and it was rare that anyone went into town. The base was an early warning-defense base, and it had a projection room, mailroom and barbershop. There were also many female employees who married men who worked and lived on the base.

Keepsake Candles.

As one employee at the candle factory said, "Who knows? Sometimes people come back to a place they always liked or where they had good memories."

The candle factory and store gets particularly spooky around Halloween when it gets dark early, and that is also when some of the more reliable staff members reported seeing strange things.

While there, Hickcock told me that he picked up the energy of a young airman who was on his way to work. Hickcock sensed that the man had just been married and was a victim of a traffic accident. "He is still at work," Hickcock said. "I felt him in there. He has a very strong presence."

OLD MEMORIAL HOSPITAL

412 Southeast Frank Phillips Boulevard

The next story is one Maria shared with me about the Old Memorial Hospital in Bartlesville. When they built the new hospital in the 1950s, the Old Memorial Hospital became a geriatric center, and she said that she had heard there was a floor for mental patients. People on that floor often reported seeing a young girl on the stairs, and she was always very playful. Other stories about the hospital involved weird things that happened to the elevators, and most of these stories are from nurses who used to work at the hospital when it was still in operation. The hospital is vacant now, but it is definitely worth a visit. Drive by if you're looking to discover a ghost and maybe get out and walk around, too.

TOM MIX MUSEUM

721 North Delaware Street
Dewey, Oklahoma

The Tom Mix Museum was once the home of Jake Bartles. As written in the museum's history, when the railroad finally came to Bartlesville, Jake thought that it was going to run right in front of his house. However, construction started a mile west, so Dewey's downtown area ended up being moved in order to accommodate the railroad. That left Bartles high and dry, so he packed up and moved his store to another plot of land. It took him 180 days to move, and he continued to open his business every day during the move. He was also still living in the store at the time.

After Bartles finally settled, he started building the Dewey Hotel. The hotel was finished in 1899, and he and his wife moved in. They lived on the second floor.

The Tom Mix Museum.

According to one of the docents at the Tom Mix Museum, people have reported seeing lights go on and go off at the former hotel. The lights at the museum occasionally flickered as well.

The museum is particularly interesting as it outlines the life of a man named Tom Mix (1890–1940), who made over three hundred movies in his lifetime. Tom Mix was a larger-than-life idol to an entire generation of children who knew him from his *Ralston Straight Shooters Radio Show*. Saddles, tack and 1920s costumes are on display at the museum, and westerns are played daily. The museum also houses Tom Mix memorabilia, most of which are items from his various careers, which include soldier, lawman and cowboy. One item that stands out in particular is an amazing snakeskin that was part of a collection donated to the museum. And of course, there is also the "Suitcase of Death," so named because it killed Mix.

According to the story, Mix was driving a 1937 supercharged automobile at a very high rate of speed (which apparently was the speed that he normally drove) through Arizona one day. There was a construction site not too far ahead, and the bridge was out. The detour actually went down through a very shallow creek, and Mix couldn't slow down. He drove into the creek and crashed into the opposite bank. One of his two suitcases in the back of the car flew forward and hit him in the back of the head, breaking his neck. Mix crashed so hard that his car actually hit the wash and then rolled over on its top and continued to roll, but it is said that Mix was already dead at that point.

According to the museum's website, Mix was born on January 6, 1880, in Mix Run, Pennsylvania. His parents, Edwin and Elizabeth Mix, named him Thomas Hezikiah Mix. When he enlisted in the army in April 1898, he listed his name as Thomas E. Mix.

After a stint in the army, Mix moved to Guthrie, Oklahoma Territory, where he worked as a bartender and as a hand on Zack Miller's 101 Ranch. He also served as the town marshal in Dewey, Oklahoma, for a short time in 1911. While working for the 101 Ranch, Mix met a man named Selig, and soon after, he began his movie career. Mix married five times and had two children: Ruth, who was born on July 13, 1912, and Thomasina, who was born on February 12, 1922.

Tom Mix died on October 11, 1940, in the previously mentioned car accident between Tucson and Florence, Arizona.

Mix's movie career spanned twenty-six years, from 1909 through 1935. At various times, he was under contract with Selig, Fox, Film Booking Office, Universal and Mascot. He starred in 336 feature films, produced 88 films, wrote 71 screenplays and directed 117 movies. He made only 9 feature films with sound, and he also starred in the fifteen-chapter serial *Miracle Rider*. Mix's movies were famous for being fast-action films that featured daredevil stunts. Tom and Tony, his horse, performed their own stunts too. In fact, Tom was a superb athlete and kept himself in great physical condition. He pioneered many of the early movie stunts, not using trick cameras or fake scenes, which worked out well since many of his films were produced on a budget.

It's possible that Mix is hanging around the museum still trying to figure out what happened. The Suitcase of Death was designed so that it

The Suitcase of Death.

could be carried around in the oil field without getting damaged. Similar suitcases are made today in Japan and cost about $1,600 (it's more or less the Cadillac of all suitcases). That might just be reason enough for Mix to haunt his own museum.

VII

Stranger Things Still

For every strange story I heard while visiting Bartlesville, two places (not including the Labadie Mansion) constantly kept coming up: Gravity Hill and Humming Highway.

Locals have also warned me of the Caney River Monster, which resides in Johnstone Park and is best not met alone.

As a side note, I could not find anyone who had a ghost story related to the Price Tower, which was designed by Frank Lloyd Wright and was built in 1956. While in the tower, I definitely felt something strange, but it could have just been the odd orientation of the building (it was very angular and a little disorienting). I found it surprising that Frank Lloyd Wright had even built anything in Oklahoma, but this tower is 221 feet high and has nineteen stories. It is actually the tallest skyscraper that he ever designed. The building is now on the National Register of Historic Places and is currently an apartment complex and office building. It also received the American Institute of Architects' twenty-five-year award.

The building was built in a cantilever design, and there are four interior vertical shafts from which all the floors and walls project. None of the exterior walls is structural; rather, they are movable screens that rest on the horizontal cantilevered floors. The interior shafts also divide the Price Tower into four separate vertical quadrants, each with its own elevator.

The Price Tower.

If you see the tower from a distance, you will notice the oxidized louvers that provide shade for the windows. The louvers create an illusion of green branches that enhances the architectural design of a tapering tower on the nineteenth floor. Wright actually called this building "the tree that escaped the crowded forest."

The furniture inside also fits the building's motif and was also designed by Wright. Perhaps his ghost does pop in for visits at times.

GRAVITY HILL

South of Bartlesville

Gravity Hill, which is just south of Bartlesville, is a hill that appears to slope upward and allows you to put your car in neutral and roll all the way past the railroad tracks (which is about one mile). There are several stories about Gravity Hill. The most popular one seems to be about a train that collided with a school bus full of children. It is said that the ghosts of the schoolchildren will push your car out of the way of the tracks.

Another story I heard regarding Gravity Hill dates back to the 1900s. In Tulsa, the townspeople used to take young black men down to the end of the road and hang them from a big tree down there. Legend has it that the ghosts of these young men help those on the tracks push their cars back up the hill.

GETTING THERE: Take Highway 11 North past the airport and follow the road to Highway 75 toward Bartlesville. Follow that road for about thirty minutes, until you see a tractor shop on your left-hand side. Turn left and stay on that road for another three miles. You will go over a bridge and then a set of railroad tracks. Keep going straight. There will be a fork in the road and a street sign that reads "Gap Road." Go straight until you come to a curve in the road. Don't take the curve; instead, turn around and drive up a few feet. This is where you put your car in neutral and feel it being pushed up the hill.

HUMMING HIGHWAY

On the Road from Oskleda to Highway 75

It is said that there was once a cemetery in this spot and the hum that can be heard is that of the dead.

According to other stories, if you are driving at a certain speed, the road will begin to hum. Again, a cemetery is attributed to the hum. The cemetery this time is said to be a Native American burial ground, and the hum is their voices.

VIII

Wrapping It all Up

Part of having the pleasure of writing about ghosts, particularly in Bartlesville, Oklahoma, was letting folks know where to visit and find real ghosts (and perhaps some that might even be fabricated). As we have already seen, haunted places are sometimes haunted by more than just the staff, but whatever the case may be, just have a good time while ghost hunting.

Rita and ghost hunter Scott Hickcock wrap it all up.

Grave marker.

Here are two of Bartlesville's fun Halloween happenings to enjoy while visiting the city.

In 2012, Bartlesville will host its sixtieth annual Spook-A-Rama event at Kiddie Park. Attractions will include a haunted house, a mad scientist show and plenty of other thrills. There is also a costume parade for the entire family and a pumpkin patch.

For directions, event dates or more information, visit www.kiddiepark.net or call 918-336-5337.

The Bartlesville Ghost Walk is also all about a hauntingly good time. Listen to the ghost stories about historic downtown buildings and take a closer look at several local businesses rumored to have spirits roaming their halls. Listen to the haunting tales in each location to find out sordid secrets from the past. The Bartlesville Ghost Walk gives visitors a glimpse of the history and the mystery of these local landmarks.

For directions, dates or more information, visit www.downtownbartlesvilleinc.org or call 918-766-4847.

IX

Tapping In to Your Own Inner Ghost Hunter

There have been countless reports of ghosts, spirits and apparitions for centuries. Some of the best times to see ghosts and to feel the energy of an unseen thing moving through your life is during the full moon.

Featured in this chapter are excerpts from one of my books entitled *The Thirteen Moons of the Mystical Woman.*

The full moon and its mystique have been a part of our culture since time began. Long before Christianity swept the globe and religions of the Old World were defined, the moon was our guide. For many societies, it was a god (as was the sun; in fact, the sun was often associated with masculine qualities while the moon was associated with femininity). The moon still has an air of mystery about it today. Those who do not believe in paganism or the mystical often admit that they can still feel the pull of the full moon when it hangs in the sky. Police officers have even said that they anticipate more criminal activity when the moon is full. It's called the lunar effect, and there have been some studies made over the years that support this theory. It has been documented that schizophrenic patients become more erratic around the time of the full moon, and hospitals often report increased activity in emergency rooms when the moon is full.

Harnessing your energies will prepare you for ghost hunting.

So why not ghosts too?

The full moon reminds us humble humans of who we are and what we are made of, which, scientifically speaking, is 60 percent water. Since the human body is mostly water, the moon can influence us mentally, physically and spiritually.

Personally, I have always been a moon lover. When I go ghost hunting on those long, cold winter nights, when the sun sets early and the wind howls, I feel I am in my element. I feel the call of the other side and of the ghosts and spirits living around us.

Perhaps I cling to this ghostly idea because it's a part of paganism. However, if you really are serious about looking for ghosts and figuring out the best way to open up that sixth sense in your own life, all you have to do is take part in becoming a "mystical woman" (or a mystical human being). There are many ways to define the term, but perhaps defining a mystical human being based on your own beliefs and what you want to do with it is the best idea. I am a mystical woman, and that means doing good, healing the earth and taking care of the love and light that I put out and receive. We manifest our hearts' desires at all times. This section of the book will help you put the tools together to do that properly. You will become more in tune with the other realm and will be able to see ghosts and spirits that are so close yet so far away.

The mystical human being will draw good ghosts and spirits, and that is what you want to do. First and foremost, however, you should be a healer of the world, beginning with your own little universe. I personally find myself more focused on healing nature than healing people, but that still means knowing how to heal yourself, being healthy and working with the mysticism inside of you.

I feel the energy from trees, which is often associated with druids. For the past twenty-one years, I have been reading and studying in earnest to become a solitary practitioner, and I do believe in the phrase "and it harm none so mote it be" and that what you send out to the universe does comes back to you threefold, good or bad. This, more than any Christian teaching I learned in church or school, is what keeps me on the "good" path—that, and the pride I take in working hard to be the mystical human being that I know I am. I have had the bad energy hit me and hit me hard. It's not good, and it's not for me or for you, so learn to create a positive future by using the power of the full moon thirteen times each year.

With this said, learn, too, that you attract those like you. If you want to attract positive energy, be the positive energy you want in your life. I often hear about people who have had negative experiences with ghosts, and I always say it is possible that encounter happened, but I do not believe a person can draw negative energy to him or her unless he or she is emitting negative energy. So if you are really serious about looking for ghosts and ghost hunting, just remember that being positive is your best defense and don't forget to surround yourself with white light.

Working with the energy of the full moon will help draw you to the ghosts or spirits you yearn to see and interact with, as well as draw the full moon's power to make it happen. Just find the power and know that it is there—most of the time, that is all you need to create and maintain a life you will love and to pull in and work with whatever you want to work with in this realm and beyond.

Being a mystical human being, working with spirits and ghosts and tapping into the unseen in no way means that you need to give up your belief in God or that you even need to believe in more than one god.

I personally don't believe in the devil or hell, but being a mystical human being doesn't mean you can't believe in these two things. I do believe that there is evil in this universe, and I do believe that if you are not in line with love that you have more lessons to learn when you come back again. If you are very evil, you might end up in a sad place on the other side, where your soul will yearn for light energy and love. It is much easier to work out the evil and the chaos of your life while you are still alive, but then again, you wouldn't be reading this book if you weren't already on the right path full of love and light.

What I call a life review will also show you (like it or not) every person and animal you have hurt in your lifetime. This includes harming animals, strangers and, in some cases, plants and objects that you don't even think about. All of these things are alive and have an energy. Perhaps many of these objects have a different vibrational energy than you do, but that does not make the object any less important.

I believe in the moon, its strength and power and the effect that it has on the world around us and the world that is unseen. We create and draw to us what we want and need in our life. Sure, I believe the world needs both men and women; yin and yang; good and evil; male and female—balance is good, and that is what tapping into the mystical power is all about. Tapping into the other side, which, of course, will help you find the ghosts and spirits, is often just the beginning of a wonderful journey.

SAFETY WHEN GHOST HUNTING

One of the first steps to becoming a mystical human being is staying safe on your ghost-hunting journeys. It is wise to understand and utilize your seven chakras, which are energy centers located on the midline of the body. Chakras govern our psychological properties and are located from the lower part of our body, our instinctual side, to the highest part of our body, the mental side. The first chakra, the root chakra (which is associated with the color red), allows us to be physically in the moment, and when it is open, you will feel grounded and stable.

The second chakra, the sacral chakra, allows us to connect with our emotions. When open, you are able to express your feelings without becoming too emotional. You are also able to express your sexuality with ease. This chakra's associated color is orange.

The navel chakra is connected to the color yellow and allows you to be assertive, especially when in a group. When open, you feel in control and have high self-esteem; when closed, you are often passive, indecisive and too timid.

The heart chakra is green and is about love, kindness and affection. Those whose heart chakra is open are compassionate and friendly and often work well with others.

The throat chakra is blue and relates to self-expression. When open, you have no trouble expressing yourself, but when closed, you are very quiet and shy.

A very important chakra is the third eye chakra, which is about insight and visualization. When open, your intuition is good, but when closed, you tend to be very rigid in your thinking. This chakra's color is purple.

The crown chakra pertains to wisdom and being one with the universe. If this chakra is open, you are unprejudiced and aware of the world. If closed, then you are not as spiritual as you could be.

Opening these chakras every morning and learning to cleanse your energy and repel negativity will allow you to go far in the process of becoming a mystical human being. In order to open your chakras, you simply have to meditate on each one every day and consciously remember the importance of opening all seven for a balanced life.

Also remember to be conscious of the spoken word, as well as the vibrational energy levels around you. How you raise your vibrational level will affect your immediate future, depending on what you concentrate on most often.

Create a Mantra

The next step in the mystical-moon process is to create your own personal mantra and repeat it every day. This can be anything from "I am a wonderful woman and am living the best life possible" to "I am love and light"—anything you want to believe and focus on. The most important thing to remember is that you should repeat your mantra as if it is actually happening now. If you say "I want to be this or that," you will continue to "want" and never "obtain." The truth is, whatever you want to be, you already are, since all of your future energy is in the universe and is moving toward you.

It is also important to create a life path, write it down, live it, believe it and know it. Perhaps even identify with a goddess or a god that makes you feel alive and that you can resonate with on a daily basis. This god or goddess should embody the energy you would like in your life. My goddess is the Egyptian goddess Bastet, who represents joy, music, dance, health and healing. I did not find her: she found me in a dream, and she is truly the last goddess I thought I would have chosen, but she is the right one for me. I tend to like dual forces (yin and yang, for example), so I looked for a god in the same pantheon (a set of gods of a particular mythology or polytheistic religion) and chose Thoth. I later found out that Thoth also represents Mercury, the planet that rules Gemini. It makes sense that I am a writer.

FULL MOONS TO WORK BY FOR STRENGTH IN GHOST HUNTING AND BEYOND

Since Native American culture is still a big part of Bartlesville's heritage, I have listed the names that the Native Americans have given to each month's full moon. (It's worth noting that some European settlers have created their own moon names.)

Month	**Moon Name**
January	Wolf Moon
February	Snow Moon, Hunger Moon, Opening Buds Moon
March	Maple Sugar Moon, Worm Moon
April	Frog Moon, Pink Moon, Planter's Moon
May	Flower Moon, Budding Moon
June	Strawberry Moon
July	Blood Moon, Buck Moon
August	Moon of the Green Corn, Sturgeon Moon
September	Harvest Moon
October	Hunter's Moon, Moon of Falling Leaves
November	Beaver Moon
December	Cold Moon

When considering working with the full moons during the year in regard to ghost hunting, keep in mind that the moon is always waxing and waning. It's best to work under a full moon when you want the strongest energy. Moreover, this is the best time to begin projects of any kind, and before you send out the energy to work and draw ghosts and spirits into

As the sun sets, the moon rises on the horizon. This is a good time for ghost hunting.

your life, think about the reasons you are interested in this type of work. This is the one day every month that the mystical human being has the most power. Additionally, the month, day of the week and sign that the moon is in may affect your energies, and you should also pay attention to equinoxes and solstices, for each one will allow you to harness a different kind of energy.

The spring (vernal) equinox represents the first season and the beginning of new things, and so your work under the full moon during this time should also be new. This is a good time to make future plans for the rest of the year. This is also the time when night and day are the same length.

During the summer solstice, also called midsummer, the sun is at its highest and the day at its longest. This is a good time of year to consider expanding your projects, and it is recommended you work hard during these months so that you may gain later on.

During the autumn equinox, the days become shorter and the nights longer, and like the spring equinox, the amount of daylight is equal to nighttime. All the work that you have done in the previous months will now pay off. This is also a good time to reflect on your work and what you have accomplished in the past few months.

The winter solstice, or yule, as it is sometimes called, is the shortest day of the year. It then comes as no surprise that this solstice is associated with death and the end of things, all in preparation for spring. This is a time to rest and cleanse for the future.

Moon Worship Through the Ages

As previously mentioned, many early civilizations—Egyptians, Babylonians and Indians, just to name a few—worshiped the moon. All of these cultures, for the most part, believed in their ancestors and working with the dead. Of particular note are the Assyrians and the Chaldeans, who were said to have called the time of the moon-god the oldest time in the history of the world. Moon worship was, and still is, based on the idea of the four stages it goes through every month, from growth to decline, and this relates to the life cycle of human beings.

TREES, FLOWERS, PLANTS, HERB AND THEIR MEANINGS

Trees

Trees have various meanings, and as you continue on your mystical path, you will find it necessary to stop for a moment, take a breath and touch a tree. Trees can also help you determine the energies around you and recognize when a ghost energy is nearby.

Trees are also powerful allies in ghost hunting and are excellent grounding points as well. Below are some types of trees and their corresponding meanings.

Tree Name	**Meaning**
Alder	Courage
Apple	Love and health
Ash	Balance and harmony
Aspen	To overcome fear and for protection
Birch	New beginnings
Cedar	Purification
Elder	Honor
Elm	Love and the mystical woman's powers
Hawthorn	Healing and letting go of negativity
Holly	Regeneration
Juniper	Protection
Maple	Prosperity
Oak	Strength and courage
Rowan	Protection and strength with ties to the magical realm
Sandalwood	Wisdom
Willow	Emotion and healing
Yew	Regeneration and intuition

Flowers

You can use flowers to travel through the thirteen full moons on your mystical path. Here is a list of flowers and what each represents:

Flower	**Meaning**
Daffodil	Joy and success
Daisy	Innocence and joy
Dandelion	Strength
Gardenia	Love and self-confidence
Geranium	Endurance
Honeysuckle	Prosperity
Jasmine	Romantic love
Lilac	Harmony
Orchid	Fertility
Rose	Love
Sunflower	Success and fertility
Violet	Psychic realms

Plants and Herbs

Using plants and herbs in your rituals will incrcasc your chances of success. Certain plants and herbs resonate with each person, and using these plants (such as dropping pieces of an herb in candle wax) will provide you with additional energy in your search for ghosts and spirits.

Herb	**Meaning**
Basil	Purification
Chamomile	Relaxation
Fennel	Healing
Garlic	Protection
Ivy	Abundance
Lavender	Calm
Mint	Cleansing
Mistletoe	Love and protection
Mugwort	Focus
Rosemary	Purification
Sage	Cleansing
Thyme	Healing

Additional Incense and Meanings

Here are a few types of incense that are always good to have on hand. Each has a specific purpose.

COPAL: This incense is used often in the Mayan culture and carries an energy that brings in love and protection.

DRAGON'S BLOOD: Protection and purification. It's also good to have on hand to boost your energy.

FRANKINCENSE: Good for purification, meditation and celebrations of all kinds.

MYRRH: Healing and purification as well as honoring the spirit world.

SANDALWOOD: This incense is good for many things, such as peace of mind and protection.

Astrological Associations

As a mystical human being, it is important to know astrological associations and how they work. The chart on the opposite page lists the various ruling planets, colors, stones, metals and body parts associated with each sign. Astrology also affects your energy levels. For example, if a full moon falls on a Wednesday in June, someone who is a Gemini and who is undertaking a project will experience powerful energy. When all of the mystical aspects of the month align, you should be at the height of your power to ghost hunt.

Sign	Planet	Color	Stone	Metal	Associated Body Part
Aries	Mars	Red	Diamond or Ruby	Iron	Head and Forehead
Taurus	Venus	Red or Orange	Emerald	Copper	Throat, Neck and Shoulders
Gemini	Mercury	Orange	Agate	Mercury	Arms and Lungs
Cancer	Moon	Bright Yellow or Orange	Moonstone	Silver	Breasts and Stomach
Leo	Sun	Yellow	Tiger's Eye	Gold	Heart and Spine
Virgo	Mercury	Yellow or Green	Sapphire	Mercury	Intestines and Hands
Libra	Venus	Green	Opal	Copper	Kidney, Lumbar and Buttocks
Scorpio	Mars or Pluto	Blue or Green	Topaz	Iron	Genitals, Colon and Nose
Sagittarius	Jupiter	Blue	Turquoise	Tin	Hips, Thighs and Liver
Capricorn	Saturn	Indigo	Garnet	Lead	Skin, Knees, Teeth and Bones
Aquarius	Saturn or Uranus	Violet or Purple	Amethyst	Uranium	Calves and Ankles
Pisces	Jupiter or Neptune	Red or Violet	Aquamarine	Tin	Feet and Body Fluids

What It Means for Each Moon to Be in a Particular Zodiac

The moon is constantly moving through the zodiac, and this will not only affect how you as a mystical human being will relate to the moon but also your life and magick (and, of course, your ghost-hunting endeavors).

Below is a description of how each of these signs works with the full moon and affects you.

MOON IN ARIES: This is the first sign in the zodiac, and it is a good time for beginning projects. Keep in mind, however, the staying power of these projects might not be as you hope since this sign is all about quick movement and progression.

MOON IN TAURUS: This is a good time to begin any new projects, as Taurus is a stable sign, and when something begins in this sign, it is often hard to change. This is also a good time to consider the earthy beauty of all that is around you and start projects relating to finances and possessions.

MOON IN GEMINI: Gemini is a fluid sign that is concerned mainly with communication issues and having a good time. Projects that are started when the moon is in Gemini might easily ebb and flow without the constant of stability. Outside influences can also play a part in your success.

MOON IN CANCER: Cancer is about nurturing and domesticity. Family projects started at this time can be very auspicious. Family is also important to the Cancer sign, and when the moon is in Cancer, it is a good time for expanding and working on these relationships.

MOON IN LEO: Leo is a strong fire sign with an emphasis on the self. A lot of drama can occur while the moon is in Leo. Nevertheless, this is definitely a good time to focus on projects that are all about you and your needs.

MOON IN VIRGO: Virgo is a detail-oriented sign. It is a good time to not only consider ideas and projects surrounding your health but also to focus on being on time and keeping schedules.

MOON IN LIBRA: This is a good time to pursue harmonious partnerships and new social relationships. Also consider projects specifically relating to marriage or other legal matters.

MOON IN SCORPIO: Scorpio is a water sign that focuses more on the mind than emotions. This is an excellent time for self-reflection and removing unnecessary and negative influences from your life.

MOON IN SAGITTARIUS: When the moon is in Sagittarius, expect lots of adventure and success. This is also a time for personal growth.

MOON IN CAPRICORN: There is no better time to pursue stable projects than when the moon is in Capricorn, as this sign is all about structure and tradition, as well as business and career.

MOON IN AQUARIUS: Projects that are started while the moon is in Aquarius are prone to instability and unpredictability. This is a good time to assert your individuality and personal freedom.

MOON IN PISCES: Pisces is a water sign that emphasizes intuition and imagination. The best time for spiritual journeys and self-discovery is when the moon is in Pisces.

What It Means for Each Moon to Fall on a Particular Day of the Week

Every day of the week has a different energy, and depending on the day and where the moon is, you may feel particularly powerful.

SUNDAY: Ruled by the Sun. Sunday is a good time to work on projects that pertain to success, strength and healing.

MONDAY: Ruled by the Moon. This is a good day for projects that relate to healing and emotions, as well as fertility and psychic matters.

Tuesday: Ruled by aggressive Mars. Tuesdays are a good day to start new projects on subjects you are passionate about.

Wednesday: Ruled by Mercury, the planet of communication and travel. This is the best day of the week to work on projects already in progress.

Thursday: Ruled by Jupiter. Thursday is a good day to handle finances and projects pertaining to money and business.

Friday: Ruled by Venus. Friday is always the day for love spells, but friendship is also important on this day.

Saturday: Ruled by Saturn. Long-term and home projects are best saved for Saturdays.

The Color of Each Moon

It is best to use your intuition when considering the color for each month's moon. Below is a list of colors to choose for each full moon. These change from year to year, but it's always what your intuition tells you that makes it the most powerful for you as a mystical human being. It might also be a good thing to consider when thinking of the ghosts or spirits you want to attract to you in your life.

Also consider ways of incorporating the color you have chosen for each full moon into your wardrobe, home and decor. Buy flowers or light candles that are the color of the month's moon.

White: This color symbolizes protection and peace, as well as purification. This color is good for all-purpose energy and can help you connect with your spirit guide.

Green: This color symbolizes healing, fertility and prosperity and is often associated with good luck.

BROWN: This color is good for keeping one grounded and also promotes financial stability.

PINK: This color promotes emotional energy, as it symbolizes love, communication and relationships. It is also associated with personal growth and inner strength.

RED: Often associated with passion and courage, as well as sexuality and lust, this color promotes action energy.

ORANGE: A symbol for happiness and positivity, this color is good for improving one's social life and also acts as a stabilizing energy.

YELLOW: Those who see the moon as yellow have strong mental powers, high levels of concentration and strong wills. This color is associated with communication, joy and creativity.

PURPLE: The color purple promotes spiritual energy and symbolizes tranquility, love and healing power.

BLUE: The color blue can enhance psychic abilities and help you work with your spirit guide. It also brings in peace and harmony to difficult projects or situations.

CHOOSING THE RIGHT INCENSE FOR EACH MONTH'S MOON

Incense can also help to create a pathway to mystical experiences for the month; in this case, to help you learn more about ghosts and spirits. Here are a few options to consider, depending on what mystical project (or projects) you are working on:

Meaning	**Incense**
Dreams	Jasmine, Rose
Fertility	Musk
Health	Sandalwood, Eucalyptus, Violet, Myrrh, Gardenia, Carnation
Love	Jasmine, Rose, Lavender, Ambergris, Amber, Neroli, Gardenia
Meditation	Jasmine, Myrrh, Magnolia, Sandalwood
Mental Power	Honeysuckle, Spearmint, Rosemary, Lilac
Money	Musk, Patchouli, Almond, Cedar, Cinnamon, Sage, Honeysuckle
Peace	Rose, Lavender, Violet, Gardenia, Narcissus
Protection	Sandalwood, Sage, Sweetgrass, Lavender, Pine, Cedar, Jasmine, Myrrh, Eucalyptus
Psychic Energy	Eucalyptus, Sandalwood, Jasmine, Lilac, Rose, Honeysuckle, Tuberose
Purification	Frankincense, Cedar, Pine, Sage, Sweetgrass, Rosemary, Myrrh, Lavender, Jasmine, Sandalwood
Sleep	Narcissus, Lavender, Rosemary
Spirituality	Sandalwood, Frankincense, Myrrh
Wisdom	Sage

A Mystical Project for January's Wolf Moon Ghost Hunt

Here's an assignment: find out what day the full moon will be on in January, consider that day and what it represents and then choose a color, incense and goddess for the month. Use your intuition: what you want and need is all about what your soul is telling you it needs to begin your mystical experiences. Also, know that you will be building on this every month during the year.

It might be worthwhile to look at the dates of the full moon on a calendar and craft a year-long plan for your mystical experiences. Since the January moon is during a time of cleansing, consider focusing on starting a new cycle in your life and getting rid of what you do not need. Start a paint project in a room in your home that needs new energy and life using the ideas described in this chapter. Saturday is a good day to work on home projects, and if the full moon falls on a Saturday, more positive energy will be put in the project.

Next, light incense or a candle and write an incantation, naming what you want; be as specific as possible. I usually end all of my incantations with "and it harm, none so mote it be" to ensure that I am allowing the energy I put out to work my request in a way that is best for me. The universe always knows what you need for your life and what lessons you are working on in this lifetime.

When the incantation is complete, snuff out the candle with your finger or fan the air above the flame until the fire is extinguished. Next, bury the piece of paper that you wrote the incantation on in the ground along with the incense stick and candle wax. (It's best to allow thc candle to burn down as much as possible. Bury whatever is left with the aforementioned items.)

You can actively practice your ability to see and feel ghosts and spirits in your life every month. Here's an example of how you can get in touch with your mystical side.

January's full moon will infuse you with an energy unlike the other moons you will experience during the year. It's then recommended that you use this energy to create what you want to discover for yourself during the year. Remember, January is the time of the year for cleansing, so get rid of unnecessary things and make room for what you really want and need.

One way to cleanse yourself is to write down all the objects, people and ideas that you need to let go of. You can even include ghosts you want to get rid of (this is especially useful for cleansing your home if you have a negative ghost energy hanging around). Since January is in Capricorn until the twenty-first of the month and because Capricorn is an earth sign, it's recommended that you get rid of unwanted things by using earth energy. Bury the paper with the unwanted list in the ground and forget about it.

LAW OF MAGICK WHEN WORKING WITH GHOSTS AND SPIRITS AS A MYSTICAL HUMAN BEING

As a mystical person looking for an experience with the other side, you will want to remember that you are constantly working with energy. Whether it's energy from the moon, energy from the sun or even energy from those surrounding you every day, the cause and effect in this universe is always alive and well. Here are thirteen laws for working on projects as you create the mystical human being you want to be over the thirteen full moons throughout the year.

LAW OF KNOWLEDGE: To change something, you have to know what you want to change and that includes you and the energy in your universe.

LAW OF CLASSIFICATION: Recognize who you are and what is around you every day; you can change your world by changing yourself first.

LAW OF CONTACT: Energy does not die, and if it has been in contact with one thing, it will always have that contact.

LAW OF NAMES: Knowing the true name of something gives you power over it in many cases.

LAW OF CAUSE AND EFFECT: What you reap, so will you sow every time.

LAW OF KNOWLEDGE: The universe holds more than we will ever know.

LAW OF CONNECTIONS: Many things are connected and can be used in place of one another when necessary.

LAW OF THE INFINITE: The universe is powerful, and when you change your soul, you can change your world in many ways for many lifetimes.

LAW OF THE SPOKEN WORD: Words are powerful and are things.

LAW OF COMMON SENSE: What you see is what you get.

LAW OF FREE WILL: In this case, you do have a choice, and only you can make it.

LAW OF OPPOSITES: There is a yin and yang to everything in order for it to exist.

LAW OF LOVE: The most important law of all: love yourself and others without judgment.

As we come to the conclusion of this book, you have not only learned about the ghosts in Bartlesville, Oklahoma, but also a little about how to work with the energy of the many ghosts and spirits who walk among us every day. Each year, you can begin a new process of working with the full moons and create ongoing mystical experiences that will eventually catapult you into a life full of positive love and light and ongoing creation. It is important to remember that you are the energy you send out. Always keep it where you know it should be.

So Mote It Be!

About the Author

Rita Cook is a writer and editor who specializes in a variety of subjects with a special emphasis on haunted houses and ghosts. She has published three books with The History Press: *A Brief History of Fort Worth*, *Haunted Dallas* and *Haunted Fort Worth*. She is also the coauthor of *Tourist Town Guides: Fredericksburg, Texas.*

Cook is the managing editor of *Celeb Life Magazine* and editor-in-chief of *Insider Magazine*. She began her journalism career in Chicago, working at *Insider Magazine* and the *Chicago Sun Times*. Her column "Green Life" is featured in the *Dallas Morning News*, and she also writes an auto column called "Behind the Wheel" that is featured in the *Washington Times Communities.*

Cook can be heard on Mondays on *Insider Magazine Radio Show*'s featured segment "I'm Standing Here."

About the Photographer

Russell W. Dandridge is a professional photographer whose work has appeared in *Insider Magazine*, the *Dallas Morning News*, *Focus Daily News*, *Waxahachie Daily Light* and *Valley Scene Magazine*. Dandridge's photography has also been featured in *Haunted Fort Worth* and *Haunted Dallas*, also published by The History Press. He also coauthored *Tourist Town Guides: Fredericksburg, Texas* with Rita Cook. Dandridge also works as a sports photographer in the fall, highlighting Texas football games in and around Dallas.